Bern

Dor...

Published by
Landmark Publishing Ltd
Waterloo House, 12 Compton, Ashbourne
Derbyshire, England DE6 1DA

Published in the USA by
Hunter Publishing Inc
130 Campus Drive, Edison NJ 08818

Acknowledgements

My grateful thanks to all the very many people who helped me research and write this book. In particular I would like to thank Charles Webbe of the Bermuda Department of Tourism for all his invaluable assistance. I am also indebted to the Department of Tourism and the Bermuda National Trust for allowing me to use the wealth of information contained in their many brochures and leaflets.

BERMUDA

Ireland Island North
Royal Navel Dockyard
The Cat Bridge
Dockyard Wharf
Grassy Bay

Daniel's Island
Somerset Long Bay
Ireland Island South
Mangrove Bay
Skeeter's Corner
Somerset
Grey's Bridge
Boaz Island
Cobbler's Island

Springfield Libary & Gilbert Nature Reserve
Watford Bridge
Cavello Bay Whalf

Spanish Point Park
Admiralty House Park
Clarence Cove
Deep Bay

Ely's Harbour
Somerset Island
Great Sound
Devonshire Dock

Somerset Bridge
Fort Scaur
Somerset Bridge Wharf
Robinson Bay Park
Palmetto Park

Hog Bay Park
Middle Rd
Hamilton

Salt Kettle Ferry
Daniel's Wharf
Hodson's Ferry
Lower Ferry
Belmont Wharf

Port Royal Golf Course
Little Sound
Riddells Bay Golf Course
Belmont Golf Course

West Whale Bay
West Whale Bay Fort
Middle Rd
Harbour Rd
Warwick Pond
Middle Rd

South Shore Park
Grape Bay

Church Bay
Christian Bay
Sinky Bay
Gibbs Hill Lighthouse
Peel Bay
Horseshoe Bay
Chaplin Bay
Warwich Long Bay
Astwood Park
Marley Beach
Coral Beach
Elbow Beach
South Shore Rd

KEY

★ **Attractions**
★ **Parks**
⚓ **Beaches**
▶ **Golf Courses**

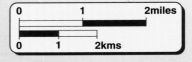

0	1	2miles

0	1	2kms

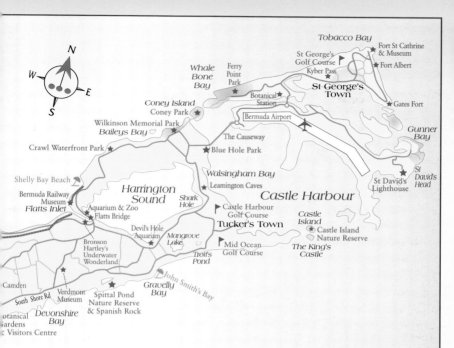

N
W   E
S

Whale Bone Bay
Ferry Point Park
Tobacco Bay
St George's Golf Course
Kyber Pass
Fort St Cathrine & Museum
Fort Albert
St George's Town
Coney Island
Coney Park
Botanical Station
Bermuda Airport
Gates Fort
Wilkinson Memorial Park
Baileys Bay
Gunner Bay
Crawl Waterfront Park
The Causeway
Blue Hole Park
Shelly Bay Beach
Walsingham Bay
Leamington Caves
St David's Head
Bermuda Railway Museum
Flatts Inlet
Harrington Sound
Shark Hole
Castle Harbour
St David's Lighthouse
Aquarium & Zoo
Flatts Bridge
Castle Harbour Golf Course
Tucker's Town
Castle Island
Devil's Hole Aquariam
Mangrove Lake
Castle Island Nature Reserve
Bronson Hartley's Underwater Wonderland
Mid Ocean Golf Course
The King's Castle
Troti's Pond
Camden
Verdmont Museum
Gravelly Bay
John Smith's Bay
South Shore Rd
Spittal Pond Nature Reserve & Spanish Rock
otanical Gardens
Devonshire Bay
c Visitors Centre

Fort St Catherine, St George

• Contents •

Feature Boxes

Note: There is parity between US & Bermudian $s. Therefore a $ price in this book may be taken as either.

1 BEFORE YOU GO

It doesn't matter how many times one visits Bermuda one is always struck at just how beautiful the island is. It is a wealth of greenery, beautiful gardens, manicured hedgerows and lawns, and gaily pastel tinted coral stone cottages with their white roofs that sparkle under a dazzling blue sky. The

Bermudians are rightly proud of their island from the well kept roads to the absence of litter, from their historic traditions to the fabulous pink sand beaches, turquoise seas and coral reefs. The whole island has a picture card beauty that it is only matched by the genuine warmth of the welcome you receive.

For more than 100 years tourism has been the mainstay of this lovely island which prides itself on its standards of service, accommodation and amenities. Bermuda's romance and charm attract thousands of honeymooners every year, and hundreds of thousands of other visitors. There is a wealth of land and water based sporting activities, world class shopping, gourmet dining and a lively nightlife. It is little wonder that many visitors to Bermuda return time and time again.

Did you know?

Bermuda's first newspaper was printed on 17 January, 1784. In 1901 camps were set up on islands in the Great Sound to house Boer prisoners of war. In 1908 the first automobile took to the roads in Bermuda. In 1944 women got the vote and in 1978 the first set of traffic lights were switched on in Hamilton.

When to Go

Temperatures do not vary a great deal throughout the year, low rainfall is distributed pretty evenly throughout the year, and any time is a good time to visit.

Getting to Bermuda

By Air

Non stop flights from Washington, Boston and New York take two hours or less and it is a seven hour flight from London.

From the US

American Airlines fly direct from New York's JFK airport, Continental Airlines from Newark, Delta from Boston and Atlanta, Kiwi International from Newark during the summer, and US Airways from Baltimore–Washington, Boston, Charlotte, Philadelphia and New York's La Guardia. All the major carriers have connecting flights to cities throughout the US.

From Canada

Air Canada flies daily direct from Toronto and weekly from Halifax with connecting flights throughout Canada.

From the UK and Europe

British Airways operated direct flights from London's Gatwick and Condor fly from Frankfurt with same day connections.

The main gateway is Bermuda International Airport on St George's about 9 miles (14km) from the capital Hamilton. There are taxis to meet all flights and regular buses during the day to the towns of St George's and Hamilton. A taxi to Hamilton should cost about $25 – $30, to St George's about $10 and to Somerset and the west end about $60.

By Sea

Bermuda is a favorite destination for cruise ships between January and November, and many stay in port – Hamilton, St George's or King's Wharf, Royal Naval Dockyard – for several days. There are many week long cruises from New York which involve two days sailing to and from Bermuda and up to four days in port.

Main cruise companies are:

Celebrity Cruises operates out of New York from April to October with cruise ships calling at Hamilton and St George's, or Somerset.

Cunard Line has several five day cruises from New York with the Queen Elizabeth 11 calling at Hamilton.

Kloster Cruise sails from New York between May and October and calls at St George's and Hamilton.

Majesty Cruise Line sails weekly from Boston between May & October calling at St George's.

Norwegian Cruise Line sails from New York between April and October and calls at St George's and Hamilton.

Royal Caribbean Cruise Line sails every Sunday from May to October and calls at St George's and Hamilton.

Regal Cruises and **Holland America Line** also include Bermuda in their cruising itineraries.

Location and Landscape

Bermuda is not one island but an archipelago of 181 named islands and islets. There are 7 main islands while some of the others are not much bigger than large rocks breaking the surface. The nearest landfall is Cape Hatteras in North Carolina which is 600 miles (966km) to the west. Bermuda is 774 miles (1241km) south east of New York, 1,415 miles (2277km) from Chicago, and more than 3,000 miles (4,828km) from London.

It is in the western North Atlantic Ocean and is not in any way associated with any part of the Caribbean or West Indies. Bermuda covers an area of 21 square miles (55 sq km), and the archipelago is 24 miles (39km) long and on average less than one mile (1.6km) wide. The main islands, shaped like a fish hook, are connected by

• HOT SPOTS •

Historic Hamilton and lively Front Street

St George's Town

Royal Naval Dockyard

Horseshoe Beach plus all the other lovely pink sand beaches

Gibbs Hill Lighthouse

Springfield and Gilbert Nature Reserves

Aquarium, Museum and Zoo

Botanical Gardens

Waterville

Verdmont

Below: The many East End beaches offer safe swimming & excellent snorkeling
Opposite page: Clocktower building, Royal Dockyard

bridges and causeways, and generally treated as one entity and collectively referred to as Main Island or Great Bermuda, which is about 22 miles (35.4km) long and has a maximum width of about 2 miles (3km) wide. Until 1940 they covered an area of 19.3 sq miles (49 sq km), but this was increased when the US Government reclaimed some land from the sea for an air base. The main islands now occupy an area of 20.5sq miles (52 sq km). About 20 of the islands are inhabited and the capital is Hamilton, with the overwhelming majority living on Great Bermuda. The other main islands are Boaz, Ireland, Somerset, St David's and St George's – all joined by bridges or causeway.

The islands are volcanic in origin, and the flattened tops of a submerged extinct volcanic mountain range that rises for more than 14,000 feet (4268m) from the ocean floor. Over the millenia a huge layer of limestone was deposited on the volcanic rock as millions upon millions of sea creatures died, sank to the sea bed and were eventually compressed into rock. As a result of further uplift, the tops of the submarine mountain range emerged above the surface of the water. The limestone layer is more than 200 feet (61m) thick in places and over huge periods, the seeping rain water has carved out huge caverns. Today, Bermuda has one of the highest concentration of limestone caves in the world. On top of the rock is a shallow layer of fertile soil. Although it only has an average depth of 6 inches (15cm) this ranges from almost nothing on exposed elevated areas to a few feet thick in lowland areas.

As a result of the warming effects of the Gulf Stream the islands are surrounded by coral reefs, making them the most northerly islands in the world with coral deposits. The islands generally consist of low rolling hills with Town Hill in Smith's Parish the highest point at 259 feet (79m). There are no rivers or freshwater lakes because of the porous limestone, and surface water quickly drains away.

History

Exactly when Bermuda was 'discovered' by Europeans remains a mystery but they were known by 1510 and La Bermuda is first recorded on a map in 1511 when Peter Martyr's Legatto Babylonica was published.

Spanish navigator Ferdinand d'Oviedo sailed close by the islands in 1515 and referred to them in his log. He credited their discovery to Spaniard Juan Bermudez, after whom they are named, although even mystery surrounds this. There are stories that Bermudez was shipwecked and cast ashore some time between 1503 and 1509 but there is no evidence to support this, although Bermudez was certainly captain of a Spanish galleon that sailed these waters in the first decade of the 16th century.

Although named Bermuda, the islands were more commonly called the Isles of Devils by early explorers and mariners because so many ships were wrecked on the offshore reefs.

In 1527 Theodore Fernando Camelo was granted the Bermuda Islands by Philip II of Spain, and he is said to have landed to inspect them in 1543. Spanish Rock on the South Shore coastline in Smith's Parish is said to get its name because it carries a plaque with an inscription of the date 1543 and the letters 'FT', which local legend has it, are those of Camelo.

However, the flat islands surrounded by reefs did not encourage settlement, especially when there were such rich pickings to be had further south on Hispaniola and the other Spanish controlled islands.

In 1593 Englishman Henry May and some French companions were shipwrecked on the islands for five months after their French vessel foundered on the reefs, and he wrote a description of Bermuda. The men eventually sailed from the islands on a small barque they had built of cedarwood.

In 1603, a Spanish galleon commanded by Captain Diego Ramirez also nearly came to grief but the storm swept his ship over the reefs. During the next three weeks on the islands repairing his ship he wrote a detailed description of the island and mapped it, and later submitted both to the Spanish authorities in Seville.

Enter the English

In 1609 James I of England granted a second charter to the Virginia Company of London allowing them to colonize the Americas. On 2 June, a fleet was dispatched under the command of Admiral Sir George Somers with about 500 would–be settlers and Governor designate Sir Thomas Gates. On 24 July, a hurricane scattered the fleet, and the Admiral's flagship Sea Venture, ran ashore on Bermuda's reef on 28 July. One member of the ship's company wrote later in his diary that it was: "A dreadfull storme... an Hell of Darkness".(This incident was immortalised by Shakespeare in his play *The Tempest* which was written towards the end of 1610. Earlier that year an account of the shipwreck entitled *A Discovery of the Bermudas*, otherwise called the Ile of

Divels, written by Silvester Jourdan had been published in London. In Act 1, scene 2 of the play, Shakespeare refers to the 'still vexed Bermoothes").

All 150 people on board the Sea Venture, however, reached land safely and over the next 10 months, they built two large pinnaces which they named the *Deliverance* and *Patience*. On 10 May, 1610 they set sail for Virginia leaving two men behind, and they reached Jamestown safely 14 days later.

On June 19 Admiral Sir George Somers sailed again from Jamestown to Bermuda to collect provisions but he died shortly after landing on St George Island. His heart is buried in the Somers Garden. The rest of the crew decided to sail back to England while three remained on the island.

In 1612 James I extended the Virginia Company's Third Royal Charter to include Bermuda and in June, a group of 60 English settlers were dispatched aboard the *Plough* to colonize it under the command of Richard Moore, the first Governor. When they landed they were met by the three men, all well, who had remained in 1610.

Fearing attack from Spain, the settlers immediately started to build forts and the seat of Government was established on Smith's Island, but shortly after transferred to St George's

Island. The Virginia Company had hoped to find ambergris in Bermuda but there was little to be found and on 25 November, 1612 it transferred its rights to the Bermuda Company. In 1615 the Company was granted a new charter allowing it to call a General Assembly with powers to enact laws provided they were not contrary to the laws of England. In 1616, Daniel Tucker, who had been with the colonists in Virginia, became the first Governor under the new charter. The first General Assizes were held in St Peter's Church on St George's.

The following year the colony was divided into tribes (shares of land) by Richard Norwood who drew the first definitive map of Bermuda. By 1620, the colony exported 20,000lbs (over 9000kgs) of potatoes to Virginia, the first to reach the American continent. In the same year the first Bermuda Onions were planted, also to become a major export crop. The Bermuda Onion became so famous that the islanders themselves were often referred to as Onions, and a large part of the island devoted to its production was known as the Onion Patch.

Building the State House

On 1 August, 1620, the first Assembly met in St Peter's Church under Governor

Leisurely shopping along Front Street, Hamilton

Nathaniel Butler, and later that year the first stone building was erected – the State House – which still stands and is the oldest State House in the western hemisphere. The first Africans were introduced as 'indentured servants' around 1616. After slavery was legalised in 1623, African and Amerindian slaves were transported to Bermuda in large numbers, and the slave population quickly outnumbered the white settlers.

When the news of the execution of King Charles I reached the islands in 1649, the colonists refused to acknowledge Cromwell's Government, and he retaliated by banning all trade between England and Bermuda. The island's agriculture – based on beef, pork and honey – was flourishing, however, and they had a growing fishing industry, and were able to withstand the trade embargo.

In 1684 under a new charter granted by Charles II, Bermuda was jointly administered by the Crown and the Virginia Company. Its legislature is the oldest of all the British dependencies.

Into the 18th Century

For the next century, the island prospered and developed a major ship building industry. The small but fast cedar-built ships were used to export island produce and other cargoes to the Americas and Caribbean islands and eventually ship building overtook agriculture as the primary industry.

Bermudians also colonized the Turks Islands to the south and established an important salt industry, which at its peak, exported 130,000 bushels to the American colonies. To protect this wealth and because of a possible threat from the Americas a ring of forts was built around the island. Over the centuries 55 forts were built, many of which survive to some extent today.

In 1775, when the American War of Revolution broke out trade embargoes where imposed against Bermuda, but the Americans lifted them in August in exchange for gun powder. The islanders, in order to protect their trading life line, raided the powder magazine in St George's, stole 100 kegs of gunpowder and shipped them to America where they were used against British troops.

As a result, troops were sent out from Britain and in 1778, the first permanent military garrison, manned by the Royal Garrison Artillery, was established. A garrison and naval base was maintained there until the 1950s. In 1784 the Bermuda Gazette, the island's first newspaper, was published and in 1793, the town of Hamilton was incorporated, followed four years later by the town of St George. The period from 1776 to 1812 saw a major boom in the islands' economy, with 40 new vessels built in 1789 alone.

The 19ᵗʰ Century

In 1809 Ireland Island was chosen as the site for the Naval Dockyard and work started the following year.

During the War of 1812–15 between Britain and the US, English privateers used St George's to sell their captured cargoes and unload American passengers from captured ships, and when the British burned Washington in 1814, they launched their attack from Bermuda.

On 12 December, 1814 the last session of the General Assembly was held in St George's; in January, 1815 the capital was moved to Hamilton and in 1817 work started on the Sessions House.

While slave trading in all British colonies was outlawed in 1807, the use of slaves was not made illegal until 1834. In 1849 the island was hit by the Great Drought, and the Black Watch Well on the North Shore in Pembroke was dug by a detachment of the Black Watch Regiment.

Bermuda played a crucial role in the American Civil War (1861–5) when ships would gather off the islands before running the gauntlet to beat the Union blockade of the southern ports. It was a time of great island prosperity.

The first tourists

The first glimmerings of tourism were seen in 1852 when work on the Hamilton Hotel began and in 1860 following the inauguration of steamship services which allowed island produce to be shipped to New York and tourists to escape the North American winters. In 1885 the Princess Hotel opened, and by the end of the century, tourism was the island's most important industry. Mark Twain a frequent visitor, said of Bermuda: "It is the right country for a jaded man to loaf in".

Between 1900 and 1902 during the Boer War, the British used islands in the Great Sound as prisoner-of-war camps, while during the First World War, several Bermuda contingents went overseas to fight for the British Empire. The tourist industry got a further shot in the arm in 1920 when the Furness–Withy Steamship Company started services. In 1923, work on the Bermudiana Hotel began, and in 1930 construction was started on the Castle Harbour Hotel.

During the Prohibition in the 1920s, Bermuda also had a

healthy trade in smuggling rum into the US. Bermuda's first train ran on 31 Octrober, 1931 on 21 miles (34km) of track from the eastern end of St George's to the western end of Somerset. It started to lose money during the Second World War and was taken over by the Government in 1946 who sold it to British Guiana, now Guyana, and allowed cars to be used on Bermuda instead.

In 1941 Churchill granted the US a 99-year lease for naval and air bases on Bermuda in return for destroyers which were desperately needed to protect the Atlantic Convoys. Fort Bell was developed partly on reclaimed land, and as a result, the Royal Naval Dockyard was closed in 1951 and the massive dry dock towed back to the UK. The British garrison was finally withdrawn in 1954, and both the Royal Navy and the US Naval Air Station had ceased operations by 1995. NASA has had a tracking station on the island since 1959. In 1953 Bermuda was the venue of the Big Three Conference, when British Prime Minister Sir Winston Churchill, US President Dwight D. Eisenhower, and French Prime Minister M. Joseph Laniel, met at the Mid Ocean Club in Tuckers Town, and in 1961 it was the venue of

The Cenotaph & Cabinet Building, Front Street, Hamilton

a summit between British PM Harold Macmillan and US President John F. Kennedy.

Politics

In 1963 the first general election under universal adult suffrage was held and the predominantly black Progressive Labour Party (PLP), the islands' first political party was formed. It called for total independence from Britain. The following year the United Bermuda Party (UBP), which was predominantly white, was launched.

This was a period of political and social upheaval with strikes and rioting and this led to a new constitution in 1968 which granted the islands much greater self determination, although this did not resolve the underlying unrest. In the 1968 general election, the first under the new Constitution, the United Bermuda Party, led by Sir Henry Tucker had a landslide victory.

In December 1971, Sir Henry Tucker resigned and was replaced by Sir Edward Richards, the first black Government leader.

In 1972 Police Commissioner George Duckett was shot and killed and in March, 1973 the Governor Sir Richard Sharples and his aide were assassinated leading to a state of emergency. Bank robber Erskine Burrows was later found guilty of all the murders and executed.

The 1980s and 1990s have been a time of steady growth and increasing prosperity. Reservoirs of water were found in several places under the islands making them self-sufficient. In 1985 Bermuda celebrated its 375th Anniverary, and in 1989 Mrs Ann Cartwright Decouto become the island's first female Deputy Premier.

The PLP continues in opposition to the ruling United Bermuda Party which in August, 1995 called a referendum to determine the issue of independence. Although the PLP urged supporters to boycott the poll, two thirds of those voting were against independence from Britain.

In March 1997, the Hon. Pamela Felicity Gordon was sworn in as Prime Minister as head of the UBP. In the October, 1998 General Election, however, the Progressive Labour Party swept into power ending the Consevative United Bermuda Party's 30-year rule.

The PLP, led by Jennifer Smith, won 26 of the 40 seats in parliament.

Climate

Bermuda has a delightful climate which is one of its great attractions. The weather is mild because of the Gulf Stream which flows between the islands and the US so it is never too hot or too cold. Bermuda has two seasons – a hot summer from May to mid-November, and a long warm autumn, winter and spring all rolled into one during the rest of the year. There are discernible seasonal changes in mid–November and December, and again in late March and April as the weather cools slightly and then heats up again.

The hottest period is July to September, with August being the hottest month. Average temperatures can be around 85°F (29.5°C). February is the coolest month when night time temperatures dip to about 57°F (14°C), although average temperatures from mid-December to late March are 70°F (21°C). Humidity is generally high throughout the year and averages about 77%. There is usually a welcome cooling breeze, especially during the evening.

There is no rainy season, and rainfall is distributed fairly evenly throughout the year at between 55 and 60 inches (140 and 152cm). In the last 100 years of records, there has never been more than 89.4 inches (226cm) in any year or less than 39 inches (102cm). While showers can be torrential, the rain seldom lasts for long and the sun is soon out to dry everything.

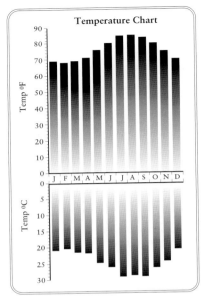

Water Supplies

Rainfall is the islands' main source of drinking water and is collected from the stepped roofs of almost every building and stored in underground tanks. It is worth taking a closer look at the roofs because the tiles are arranged in such a way that the rain water is chanelled down in a series of hairpin bend-like gulleys to the down pipes which take the water to the storage tanks. The roofs are painted white and kept spotlessly clean so as not to dirty the water.

Supplementary supplies are also drawn from other underground areas, purified and piped to hotels, guest houses, hospitals, commercial properties and some homes. Large hotels outside the water mains distribution system have desalination or reserve osmosis systems to provide drinking water. Not many years ago, the islands had to ship in water in times of drought, but reserves have been developed to such an extent that this is no longer necessary. The sitation continues to improve with more major desalination facilities planned.

Hurricane season lasts from June to November with September and October usually the busiest months for tropical storms. Tropical storms are well monitored, and in reality, most do not make landfall, but if a hurricane threatens, follow the advice given locally. There are detailed hurricane action plans designed to protect both people and property.

The Bermuda Triangle

The legendary Bermuda Triangle is a section of the North Atlantic where more than 50 ships and 20 airplanes are said to have mysteriously disappeared. The Triangle is said to run from the southern coast of the United States out to Bermuda and then down to the Greater Antilles, the northernmost of the Caribbean Islands.

The first recorded tales about mysterious happenings in this area date from the mid-19th century when some ships were discoverd abandoned but undamaged, and others were reported to have sent out distress messages and then simply vanished. More recently US naval aircraft are said to have simply disappeared from the radar screen as they crossed the area never to be seen again. It is quite probable that many of the earlier incidents were the result of piracy which was rife in the area. Lone ships were easy prey and crews would be killed and thrown overboard into the shark infested waters so there would be no witnesses. The ships would then be set adrift or scuttled.

Whatever the origin of the legend, two things are certain. No wreckage has ever been found to substantiate claims of missing ships or aircraft, and every year tens of thousands of vessels and planes cross the area without mishap.

The People

Bermuda's population is a multicultural patchwork of many nationalities. The majority of the people are descended from African slaves brought to the island before Britain outlawed the slave trade in 1807. There are significant populations of Britons and Portuguese, the latter descendants of labourers who largely came from Madeira and the Azores

City Hall, Hamilton

in the mid-19th century to supplement the work force after Emancipation. As a result while English is the main language some Portuguese is still spoken.

In 1911 Bermuda had a population of 18,994 of which 12,303 were black and 6,691 white. In 1960 the population had risen to 42,640 – 26,683 black and 15,957 white, and the last census showed a population of 58,460, of whom 35,630 were black and 22,830 white. Today the year round population is about 61,000.

Culture

Bermuda has a strong artistic tradition with a wide range of theatre, music and dance. There is the City Hall Theatre in Hamilton; the Jabulani Repertory Company; Bermuda Musical and Dramatic Society; Bermuda Society of Arts; Bermuda Philharmonic Society; Bermuda Gombey Troupes; Bermuda Civic Ballet; Dance Theatre of Bermuda and the Gilbert and Sullivan Society of Bermuda.

The multi-national heritage of Bermuda has led to many imported traditions such as the very British afternoon tea and cricket, Scottish Highland dancing, Gombey Dancers from Angola in Africa and kite flying on Good Friday. It is also reflected in the island's music which ranges from church choirs to string quartets and Gilbert and Sullivan to Gombey and Calypso. Legendary Calypso stars include the Talbot Brothers, Joe 'Conchshell' Benjamin, Stan 'Lord Necktie' Seymour and the 'Bermuda Strollers'.

The **Gombey Dancers** combine traditions from Africa, the West Indies and Britain, and combine elements of song, dance, theatre and mime. The troupe, known as a 'crowd' is led by the elaborately dressed Captain, and the whole performance is highly stage managed following traditional themes. There are Chiefs and Warriors known as Choppers because of the tomohawks they carry, and the Trapper who is in endless unsuccessful pursuit of an Indian. Many of the dances whether solos, duets and ensemble re-enact tales of combat, usually representing the struggle between good and evil, such as the battle between David and Goliath, the struggle of the slaves for emancipation and so on.

Many famous artists and sculptors have been born in or inspired by Bermuda, and these include Desmond Fountain, Michael Swan, Winslow Homer, Andrew Wyeth, Georgia O'Keefe, Charles Demuth, Marl Emmerson, Joan Forbes, Jill Amos Raine, Robert Bassett and Sharon Wilson.

The Economy

Bermuda's economy is based largely on tourism and internationally financial services, and it is one of the world's leading offshore financial centers. A significant proportion of the island's revenue also comes from US forces based there. The gross national product per head of the population is the highest in the West Indies and continues to grow.

Agriculture is not a major industry with most food imported, although bananas, citrus fruit and vegetables are grown commercially and there are herds of dairy cattle. Some sand and limestone is excavated for local construction, and there are some light industries, mostly connected with pharmaceuticals, printing and paint.

Tourism is the main industry and the major employer, but a growing number of financial institutions, especially investment houses and insurance companies, have offices in Bermuda because of its zero income tax.

The Government and Judiciary

Bermuda is a self-governing British colony with a parliamentary government elected every 5 years. The British monarch is head of state and represented on the island by the Governor. Executive power is in the hands of the Prime Minister, the leader of the majority party in parliament, who appoints a Council of Ministers. The legislature consists of the House of Assembly with 40 elected members and the Senate, whose members are appointed by the Governor, the Prime Minister or the leader of the opposition.

Plant and animal life

The islands have a rich subtropical vegetation with many beautiful flowering plants and trees. The mild, humid climate and heavy dews, particularly in summer, offer ideal growing conditions and as many as three crops a year are harvested in some vegetable gardens. The continuing need for land for housing to accommodate the island's steadily growing population, however, means that four fifths of all the food consumed in Bermuda is now imported.

For its small size, Bermuda has a large proportion of land protected as parks and reserves. It has more than 350 species of birds, and the Botanical Gardens has more than 1,000 varieties of flora, including 150 species of hibiscus.

Bermuda is a world center for breeding and species reintroduction, and renowned for marine, biological and atmospheric research.

The whole island is a flower garden 365 days a year. Purple bougainvillea flowers everywhere, there are huge hedges of hibiscus, pink oleander, scarlet Royal Poinciana, frangipani, morning glory (also known as bluebell), passion flower and Easter lilies abound. There are heliconia, also known as the lobster plant, bird of paradise flowers and anthurium. The flamboyant tree is also known as the tourist tree because it bursts into bloom during the summer and is a blaze of orange or red. There are also many species of palm trees, as well as palmetto, fiddlewood, cedar, olivewood bark, Caribbean and Screw pine, casuarina and mangrove, and at Christmas the wild poinsettias burst into bloom. Gardens and hedgerows ab-ound with morning glory and Mexican poppy, nasturtium, freesia and Bermudiana. You can spot yucca, Natal Palm, Darrell's Fleabane, Surinam cherry and paw paw, as well as bananas, loquat and cassava.

Along the coast there are areas of almost impenetrable mangroves. Beach morning glory with its array of pink flowers is found on many beaches, and is important because its roots help prevent sand drift. The plant also produces nectar from glands in the base of its leaf stalks which attract ants, and it is thought this evolution has occurred so that the ants will discourage any leaf-nibbling predators. Other beach plants include seagrape and the manchineel, which should be treated with caution.

Note

The manchineel, which can be found on Some beaches, has a number of effective defensive mechanisms which can prove very painful. Trees vary from a few feet to more than 30 feet (9m) in height, and have widely spreading, deep forked boughs with small, dark green leaves and yellow stems, and fruit like small, green apples. If you examine the leaves carefully without touching them, you will notice a small pin-head sized raised dot at the junction of leaf and leaf stalk. The apple-like fruit is poisonous, and sap from the tree causes very painful blisters. Sap is released if a leaf or branch is broken, and more so after rain. Avoid contact with the tree, don't sit under it, or on a fallen branch, and do not eat the fruit. If you do get sap on your skin, run into the sea and wash it off as quickly as possible.

Another unwelcome resident is the Portuguese Man O'War, especially between March and July. Warning signs are posted on beaches most likely to be affected.

Marine Life

Of course, the sea teems with brilliantly marked fish and often, even more spectacularly marked coral and marine plants. Even if you just float upside down in the water with a face mask on, you will be able to enjoy many of the beautiful underwater scenes, but the best way to see things is by scuba diving, snorkeling or taking a trip in a glass bottomed boat.

There are scores of different corals that make up the reefs offshore. Coral, like the tropical rain forests, is essential in helping to regulate the earth's atmosphere, by acting as a 'carbon sink'. Both coral and the trees in the rain forests are able to absorb carbon dioxide from the atmosphere. If coral reefs are destroyed and tropical rain forests felled, carbon dioxide levels increase resulting in the 'green house effect' and the threat of global warming. Ironically, if temperatures were to rise globally by just a few degrees, the polar ice caps would thaw faster, ocean levels would rise, and most of the low-lying islands of

Bermuda would be submerged. Warmer water temperatures would also kill the remaining coral and have a devastating effect on marine life.

There are hard and soft corals and only one, the white tipped fire coral poses a threat to swimmers and divers, because if touched, it causes a stinging skin rash. Among the more spectacular corals are deadman's fingers, staghorn, brain coral and seafans, and there are huge sea anemones and sponges, while tropical fish species include the parrotfish, blue tang surgeonfish, tiny but aggressive damselfish, angelfish and brightly marked wrasse. Whales and dolphins can also be seen offshore.

Animal Life

The animal life is sparse with no large animals, and the wildlife mainly consists of lizards, anoles, skinks, giant toads, very noisy frogs and land crabs, especially among the mangroves, and birds. The largest of the lizards is the Warwick lizard which can grow up to 14 inches (35cm) long.

Birds

Because of its location stuck out in the Atlantic, Bermuda plays host to large numbers of migratory birds every year, several of them rare species. Many of the

Bermuda is one large
tropical garden

indigenous species of birds have died out. You will see, however, the beautiful satin white Bermuda long tail (or white tailed tropic bird), Eastern bluebird, striking red cardinals, white eyed vireo (chick of the village), and yellow kiskadee. The Bermuda petrol or cahow, was thought to have been extinct for 300 years until it was rediscovered in 1951 and it is now one of the rarest birds in the world. The females lay only one egg a year and spend most of their time soaring over the oceans.

Offshore you may see the magnificent frigatebird, easily recognisable by its size, long black seven foot (2m) wing span, forked tail and apparent effortless ability to glide on the winds. There are brown booby birds, named by sailors from the Spanish word for 'fool' because they were so easy to catch. Pelicans which look so ungainly on land, yet are so acrobatic in the air, can be seen as well as laughing gulls and royal terns. Several species of sandpiper can usually be seen scurrying around at the water's edge.

If you are really interested in bird watching, pack a small pair of binoculars. The new mini-binoculars are ideal for island bird watching, because the light is normally so good that you will get a clear image despite the small object lens.

Plants

As most of the plants, fruits, vegetables and spices will be new to the first time visitor, the following brief descriptions are offered. Not all are grown on the islands but most are served or can be bought: **Bananas** are one of the Caribbean's most important exports, thus their nickname 'green gold'.

There are three types of banana plant; the banana that we normally buy in supermarkets originated in Malaya and were introduced into the Caribbean in the early 16th century by the Spanish. The large bananas, or plantains, originally came from southern India, and are largely used in cooking. They are often fried and served as an accompaniment to fish and meat. The third variety is the red banana, which is not grown commercially and still quite rare but you might see them growing in a back yard.

Most banana plantations cover only a few acres and are worked by the owner or tenant, although there are still some very large holdings. A banana produces a crop about every nine months, and each cluster of flowers grows into a hand of bananas. A bunch can contain up to twenty hands of bananas, with each hand having up to 20 individual fruit.

Although they grow tall, bananas are not trees but

herbacious plants which die back each year. Once the plant has produced fruit, a shoot from the ground is cultivated to take its place, and the old plant dies. Bananas need a lot of attention, and island farmers will tell you that there are not enough hours in a day to do everything that needs to be done. The crop needs fertilising regularly, leaves need cutting back, and you will often see the fruit inside blue tinted plastic containers, which protect it from insect and bird attack, and speed up maturation.

Breadfruit

The breadfruit is a cheap carbohydrate-rich food, although pretty tasteless when boiled. It is best eaten fried, baked or roasted over charcoal. The slaves did not like them at first, but the tree spread and

Captain Bligh

Breadfruit was introduced to the Caribbean by Captain Bligh in 1793. He brought 1200 breadfruit saplings from Tahiti aboard the *Providence*, and these were first planted in Jamaica and St Vincent, and then quickly spread throughout the islands. It was Bligh's attempts to bring in young breadfruit trees that led to the mutiny on the *Bounty* four years earlier.

Bligh was given the command of the 215 tons (219 tonnes) *Bounty* in 1787 and was ordered to take the bread fruit trees from Tahiti to the West Indies where they were to be used to provide cheap food for the slaves. The ship had collected its cargo and had reached Tonga when the crew under Fletcher Christian mutinied. The crew claimed that Bligh's regime was too tyranical, and he and 18 members of the crew who stayed loyal to him, were cast adrift in an open boat. The cargo of breadfruit was dumped overboard. Bligh, in a remarkable feat of seamanship, navigated the boat for 3,600 miles (5800 km) until making landfall on Timor in the East Indies. Some authorities have claimed that it was the breadfruit tree cargo that sparked the mutiny, as each morning the hundreds of trees in their heavy containers had to be carried on deck, and then carried down into the hold at nightfall. It might have proved just too much for the already overworked crew.

can now be found almost everywhere. It has large dark, green leaves, and the large green fruits can weigh 10-12lbs (4-6 kg). The falling fruits explode with a loud bang and splatter its pulpy contents over a large distance. It is said that no one goes hungry when the breadfruit is in season.

Calabash

Calabash trees are native to the Caribbean and have huge gourd like fruits which are very versatile when dried and cleaned. They can be used as water containers and bowls, bailers for boats, and as lanterns. Juice from the pulp is boiled into a concentrated syrup and used to treat coughs and colds, and the fruit is said to have many other medicinal uses.

Cocoa

Cocoa is another important crop, and its Latin name theobroma means 'food of the gods'. A cocoa tree can produce several thousand flowers a year, but only a fraction of these will develop into seed bearing pods. It is the heavy orange pods that hang from the cocoa tree which contain the beans which contain the seeds that produce cocoa and chocolate.

The beans, containing a sweet, white sap that protects the seeds, are split open and kept in trays to ferment. This process takes up to eight days and the seeds must be kept at a regular temperature to ensure the right taste and aroma develops. The seeds are then dried. In the old days people used to walk barefoot over the beans to polish them to enhance their appearance. Today, the beans are crushed to extract cocoa butter, and the remaining powder is cocoa. Real chocolate is produced by mixing cocoa powder, cocoa butter and sugar.

You can sometimes buy cocoa balls in the markets which make a delicious drink. Each ball is the size of a large cherry. Simply dissolve the ball in a pan of boiling water, allow to simmer and then add sugar and milk or cream, for a rich chocolate drink. Each ball will make about four mugs of chocolate.

Coconut

Coconut palms are everywhere and should be treated with caution. Anyone who has heard the whoosh of a descending coconut and leapt to safety, knows how scary the sound is. Those who did not hear the whoosh, presumably did not live to tell the tale. Actually, very few people do get injured by falling coconuts and that is a near miracle in view of the tens of thousands of palms all over the island, but it is not a good idea to picnic in a coconut grove!

Coconut trees are incredibly hardy, able to grow in sand and even when regularly washed by

Spanish Port

The Coconut Husk

The coconut, bought in shops, is the seed with its layer of coconut surrounded by a hard shell. This shell is then surrounded by a layer of copra, a fibrous material, and this is covered by a large green husk. The seed and protective coverings can weigh 30lbs (13.5 kg) and more. The seed and casing is waterproof, drought proof and able to float, and this explains why coconut palms which originated in the Pacific and Indian Oceans, are now found throughout the Atlantic – the seeds literally floated across the seas.

The coconut palm is extremely versatile. The leaves can be used as thatch for roofing, or cut into strips and woven into mat and baskets, while the husks yield coir, a fibre resistant to salt water and ideal for ropes and brushes and brooms. Green coconuts contain a delicious thirst-quenching 'milk', and the coconut 'meat' can be eaten raw, or baked in ovens for two days before being sent to processing plants where the oil is extracted. Coconut oil is used in cooking, soaps, synthetic rubber and even in hydraulic brake fluid.

As you drive around the island, you might see groups of men and women splitting the coconuts in half with machetes preparing them for the ovens. You might also see halved coconut shells spaced out on the corrugated tin roofs of some homes. These are being dried before being sold to the copra procressing plants.

salty sea water. They can also survive long periods without rain. Their huge leaves, up to 20 feet (6m) long in mature trees, drop down during dry spells so a smaller surface area is exposed to the sun which reduces evaporation. Coconut palms can grow up to 80 feet (24m) tall, and produce up to 100 seeds a year. The seeds are the second largest in the plant kingdom, and these fall when ripe.

Dasheen

Dasheen is one of the crops known as 'ground provisions' in the Caribbean, the others being sweet potatoes, yams, eddo and tannia. The last two are close relatives of dasheen, and all are members of the aroid family, some of the world's oldest cultivated crops. Dasheen with its 'elephant ear' leaves, and eddo grow from a corm which when boiled thoroughly can be used like potato, and the young leaves of either are used to make calaloo, a spinach-like soup. Both dasheen and eddo are thought to have come from China or Japan but tannia is native to the Caribbean, and its roots can be boiled, baked or fried. It grows wild in The Bahamas but is not generally used for food.

Guava

Guava is common throughout the West Indies, and the aromatic, pulpy fruit is also a favorite with birds who then distribute its seeds. The fruit bearing shrub can be seen on roadsides and in gardens, and it is used to make a wide range of products from jelly to 'cheese', a paste made by mixing the fruit with sugar. The fruit which ranges from a golf ball to a tennis ball in size, is a rich source of vitamin A and contains lots more vitamin C than citrus fruit.

Mango

Mango can be delicious if somewhat messy to eat. It originally came from India but is now grown throughout the Caribbean and found wherever there are people. Young mangoes can be stringy and unappetising, but ripe fruit from mature trees which grow up to 50 feet (15m) and more, are usually delicious, and can be eaten raw or cooked. The juice

is a great reviver in the morning, and the fruit is often used to make jams and other preserves. The wood of the mango is often used by boatbuilders.

Nutmeg

Nutmeg trees are found on all the Caribbean islands. The tree thrives in hilly, wet areas and the fruit is the size of a small tomato. The outer husk, which splits open while still on the tree, is used to make the very popular nutmeg jelly. Inside the seed is protected by a bright red casing which when dried and crushed, produces the spice mace. Finally, the dark outer shell of the seed is broken open to reveal the nutmeg which is dried and then ground into a powder, or sold whole so that it can be grated to add flavor to dishes.

Passion fruit

Passion fruit is not widely grown but it can usually be bought at the market. The pulpy fruit contains hundreds of tiny seeds, and many people prefer to press the fruit and drink the juice. It is also commonly used in fruit salads, sherbets and ice creams.

Pawpaw or papaya trees

Pawpaw or papaya trees are also found throughout the is-

Continued on page 36...

Replica of the Deliverance,
St George's

land and are commonly grown in gardens. The trees are prolific fruit producers but grow so quickly that the fruit soon becomes difficult to gather. The large, juicy melon-like fruits are eaten fresh, pulped for juice or used locally to make jams, preserves and ice cream. They are rich sources of vitamin A and C. The leaves and fruit contain an enzyme which tenderises meat, and tough joints cooked wrapped in pawpaw leaves or covered in slices of fruit, usually taste like more expensive cuts. The same enzyme, papain, is also used in chewing gum, cosmetics, the tanning industry and, somehow, in making wool shrink resistant. A tea made from unripe fruit is said to be good for lowering high blood pressure.

Pigeon Peas

Pigeon Peas are widely cultivated and can be found in many back gardens. The plants are very hardy and drought resistant, and are prolific yields of peas which can be eaten fresh or dried and used in soups and stews.

Pineapples

Pineapples were certainly grown in the Caribbean by the time Columbus arrived, and were probably brought from South America by the Amerindians. The fruit is slightly smaller than the Pacific pineapple, but the taste more intense.

Sugar Cane

Sugar Cane is no longer grown commercially but can be seen growing wild in some places. Most of the cane was grown to produce molasses for the rum industry. The canes can grow up to 12 feet (3.5m) tall and after cutting, the canes had to be crushed to extract the sugary juice. After extraction, the juice was boiled until the sugar crystalised. The mixture remaining was molasses and this was used to produce rum.

Sugar Apple

Sugar Apple is a member of the annona fruit family, and grows wild and in gardens throughout the islands. The small, soft sugar apple fruit can be peeled off in strips when ripe, and is like eating thick apple sauce. They are eaten fresh or used to make sherbet or drinks. Soursop, is a member of the same family, and its spiny fruits can be seen in hedgerows and gardens. They are eaten fresh or used for preserves, drinks and ice cream.

Food and Drink

The islands offer a huge choice when it comes to eating out, from excellent traditional island fare to the finest international cuisine at the best tourist hotels and elegant restaurants. There are almost 100 restaurants, cafes and pubs, and you can enjoy a terrace breakfast, an alfresco lunch, traditional afternoon tea and a romantic moonlit dinner, beach barbecue or sumptuous seafood buffet.

Dining out offers the chance to experiment with all sorts of unusual spices, vegetables and fruits, with creole and island dishes, and, of course, rum punches and other exotic cocktails

Eating out is very relaxed although many restaurants do have a dress code which requires men to wear jacket and tie, although most people like to wear something a little smarter at dinner after a day on the beach or out sightseeing. Many hotels have a tendency to offer buffet dinners or barbecues, but these can be interesting and tasty affairs.

Breakfast

Breakfast can be one of the most exciting meals of the day for a visitor. There is a huge range of fruit juices to choose from. Try a glass of water melon juice, followed by a fresh grapefruit, or slices of chilled paw–paw or mango. Most hotels offer fruit plates with a wide choice so you should be able to taste your way through them all during your stay.

These fruits also make great jams and preserves, and you can follow the fruit with piping hot toast spread with perhaps citrus marmalade or guava jam. Most tourist hotels also offer traditional American breakfasts for those who can not do without them.

Lunch

During the summer, you may find fruits such as the kenip, plumrose, sugar apple and yellow plum. Green bananas and plantains are usually eaten boiled or steamed in the skin, then cut into slices and served very hot. They also make excellent chips when fried.

Sunday brunches have become an island tradition and many hotels compete with each other to see who can offer the most sumptuous spreads. Tasty codfish and banana is a typical Sunday brunch offering, and is both very filling and nutritious.

Dinner

There is usually a good choice when it comes to dinner. **Starters** include a huge choice of fruit juices from orange and grapefruit to the more unusual ones like soursop, loquat and tamarind. You can also drink green coconut 'milk'. There is excellent soup made from the island's Bermuda onions.

Fish and clam chowders are also popular starters. Fish chowders are often spiced up with the addition of rum and sherry peppers, an island specialty. Try heart of palm, excellent fresh shrimps or scallops, smoked kingfish wrapped in crepes or crab backs, succulent land crab meat sauteed with breadcrumbs and seasoning, and served restuffed in the shell. It is much sweeter than the meat of sea crabs.

Bermuda lobster, which is really a crayfish, is delicious with a sweeter more succulent taste than Maine lobster. Lobster season is from September to the end of March, and broiled lobster is most popular because this allows the full flavors to be appreciated. Mussel pie is also excellent and an island specialty.

The fish is generally excellent, and don't be alarmed if you see dolphin on the menu. It is not the protected species made famous by 'Flipper', but a solid, close-textured flat faced fish called the dorado, which is delicious. Salt fish often appears on the menu. Salting was the most common form of food preserving, and allowed surplus catches to be safely kept until times of food shortage, or for when the seas were too rough for the fishing boats to go to sea. There is also snapper, wahoo, grouper, kingfish, redfish, jacks, balaouy, snapper, tuna, flying fish, lobster, swordfish, baby squid and mussels. On St George's Island, shark hash is a traditional dish. Try seafood jambalaya, chunks of lobster, shrimps and ham served on a bed of braised seasoned rice, shrimp creole, with fresh shrimp sauteed in garlic butter, parsley and served with tomatoes, or fish creole, with fresh fish steaks cooked in a spicy onion, garlic and tomato sauce, served with rice and fried plaintain.

Conch (pronounced 'konk') is almost the national dish and is served in scores of different ways from chowders and soups, to salads and fritters.

There are more traditional British dishes such as roast beef and Yorkshire pudding and steak and kidney pie but there are excellent curries and other ethnic cuises. From the Portuguese comes red bean soup and spicy sausage, while curried goat and roti have been introduced from 'down south', which is how the Bermudians refer to the Caribbean. Roti was brought to the island

Bermuda's most elegant mode of transport

Another note of Warning

On most tables you will find a bottle of pepper sauce. It usually contains a blend of several types of hot pepper, spices and vinegar, and should be treated cautiously. Try a little first before splashing it all over your food, as these sauces range from hot to unbearable.

If you want to make your own hot pepper sauce, take four ripe hot peppers, one teaspoon each of oil, ketchup and vinegar and a pinch of salt, blend together into a liquid, and bottle.

by East Indian indentured workers in the 19th century. It consists of a paper thin dough wrapped around a spicy hot curry mixture containing beef, chicken, vegetables or fish. The chicken roti often contains small bones which some people like to chew on, so be warned. Island fast food also includes patties, which are pastry cases stuffed with meats or saltfish, and fritters. Another Bermuda feature is the lunch wagon and you can usually find one close to the most popular beaches offering good value snacks and drinks during the day. For **vegetarians** there are excellent salads, stuffed breadfruit, stuffed squash and pawpaw, baked sweet potato and yam casserole.

Buffet

On the buffet table, you will often see a dish called pepper pot. This is usually a hot, spicy meat and vegetable stew to which may be added small flour dumplings and shrimps.

There are wonderful breads, and you should try them if you get the chance. There are banana and pumpkin breads, and delicious cakes such as coconut loaf cake, guava jelly cookies and rum cake.

For **dessert**, try fresh fruit salad, with added cherry juice, and sometimes a little rum, which is a year round popular dessert. There are a wide variety of fruit sherbets using tropical fruits such as banana, coconut, soursop, mango, sappodilla, gooseberry, pineapple and tamarind.

Or, try one of the exotically flavored ice creams. There are also banana fritters and banana flambe, coconut cheesecake, green papaya or guava shells simmered in heavy syrup. You should also try the excellent loval goat cheese. There are many seasonal specialties such as cod fish cakes and hot cross buns on Good Friday, sweet potato pie on Guy Fawke's Day, cassava pie at Christmas and peas 'n plenty on New Year's Day.

Drinks

Rum is the drink of the islands. Columbus is credited with planting the first sugar cane in the Caribbean, on Hispaniola, during his third voyage, and the Spanish called it aguardiente de cana, meaning cane liquor. The Latin name for sugar cane is saccharum, and it was English sailors who shortened this to rum. Another suggestion is that the name comes from the old English word 'trumbullion', which means a drunken brawl. It figured prominently in the infamous Triangle Trade in which slaves from Africa were sold for rum from the West Indies which was sold to raise money to buy more slaves.

Rum had such fortifying powers that General George Washington insisted every soldier be given a daily ration, and a daily tot also became a tradition in the British Royal Navy. The very strong Navy Rum was issued as a daily tot from 1655 until 1970.

The rum trade on Bermuda got a major boost during the 1920's because of the Prohibition in the United States. Rum distilled on the island was smuggled into the US and this

> ## Note
>
> While many of the main tourist hotel restaurants offer excellent service, time does not have the same urgency as it does back home, and why should it after all, as you are on holiday. Relax, enjoy a drink, the company and the surroundings and don't worry if things take longer, the wait is generally worth it.

trade continued long after the end of Prohibition. All sorts of rums are produced from light to dark and of varying strengths. Among the best is Gosling's Black Seal Rum which has been sold for more than 140 years.

Rum is aged in American white oak barrels, and the longer it remains in the barrel, the more flavor and color it absorbs. Traditionally, dark rum spent a long time ageing in barrels, and light rums only a short time. Today, most white and light rums are not aged in wood, but in stainless steel vats. The finest rums are best drunk on the rocks, but if you want to capture a bit of the Bermuda spirit, have a couple of rum punches. A classic Bermuda tipple is 'Dark and Stormy' a generous helping of Black Seal rum and ginger beer.

Bermuda Rum Swizzle:
Into a large pitcher place I teaspoon of sugar, one and half oz of lime, half an ounce of Farernum and a dash of Angostura bitters, one oz of Barbados rum and one oz of Demerara rum. Add finely chopped ice, stir vigorously and then pour into a frosted tumbler.

Plantation Rum Punch:
To make Plantation Rum Punch, thoroughly mix three ounces of rum, with one ounce of lime juice and one teaspoon of honey, then pour over crushed ice, and for a little zest, add a pinch of freshly grated nutmeg.

Most tourist hotels and bars also offer a wide range of other cocktails both alcoholic, usually very strong, and non-alcoholic. Bermuda Triangle Brewing in Southampton Parish, is a microbrewery noted for its fine beers such as Wild Hogge, Full Moon, Hammerhead and Spinnaker. North Rock Brewing Co is another micro brewery which sells its ales and beers in its tavern on South Road in Smith's Parish.

Tap water is safe to drink and mineral and bottled water is widely available, and so are soft drinks.

The Taste of Bermuda

Try some of the following recipes created by Jean-Claude Garzia, Executive Chef at Cambridge Beaches, and featured in his *A Taste of Bermuda*.

Chilled Bermuda Fruit Soup

Ingredients
2 oranges, 4 grapefruits, 1 lemon, quarter cup of sugar, half cup of water, one cup sweet white wine, 1oz Grand Marnier liqueur, 6 tablespoons of butter at room temperature and 8 loquats.

Peel the oranges and grapefruit, removing all pith and outer skin and divide into segments. Take the zest of half an orange and half a lemon and cut into thin strips (julienne). Blanch the strips for a few minutes in boiling water, drain and then caramelise them by cooking for about 10 minutes in the sugar dissolved in half a cup of water.

In a saucepan combine the wine, Grand Marnier and lemon juice, bring to the boil and reduce by half. Add the caramelised strips and with a whisk, beat in the butter, a tablespoon at a time. Arrange the fruit segments in alternate layers in serving bowls and cover with sauce, and chill in the fridge until cold. Just before serving, garnish with slices of peeled, seeded loquats.

Pawpaw flan

Ingredients
2 green pawpaws, 3 eggs, one cup heavy cream, one cup milk, pinch of nutmeg, I teaspoon of butter for greasing, and ramekin dishes.

Peel the pawpaws, remove the seeds, cut in pieces and cook, covered, in boiling water for about 20 minutes. When tender, drain and dry on absorbent paper, then puree the pieces finely in a blender or mixer.

In a deep bowl beat the egg yolks, the egg white, the cream and milk with a whisk. Add the pawpaw purée and nutmeg, season to taste and then strain through a fine sieve.

Cover the bottom of an oven proof casserole with newspaper and arrange lightly buttered ramekin dishes on the paper. Fill each dish with the paw-paw mixture and pour an inch of warm water into the casserole around the ramekins and cook at 350 degrees for 35 minutes.

To serve: allow to cool for a minute or two, then un-mould by running a small knife around the inside of each dish. About ten minutes after unmoulding, cover them with a sheet of tin foil toprevent them from becoming dry or discolored.

Bermuda Onion Pie with bacon

Ingredients
1lb pastry (any basic recipe), three and a half ounces of bacon, 6 tablespoons of butter, one tablespoon of oil, one pound of Ber-muda onions, one tablespoon of flour, one cup of heavy cream, one cup of milk, 5 mediumm eggs, beaten, a pinch of nutmeg and salt and pepper to taste.

Fry the chopped bacon over a low heat for about 5 minutes until 'limp', then drain on a paper towel. Heat 5 tablespoons of butter and the oil in a saucepan, add the onions and saute gently without browning. Sprinkle with the flour, and cook for a further 5 minutes, then remove from heat. Slowly add the cream, then the milk and finally the beaten eggs. Season with salt and pepper and add the nutmeg and beat with a whisk.

Roll out the pastry and spread in a buttered and floured tart tin or flan dish. Sprinkle the bacon over the pastry and then slowly pour in the cream mixture. Cut the remaining one tablespoon of butter into small pieces and spread on top. Bake for about 35 to 40 minutes at 375 degrees, and serve hot as an entree.

Fettucine Mangrove Bay

Ingredients
1lb fresh fettucine noodles, 3 ozs olive oil, 10 ripe medium to-matoes, freshly ground black pepper, salt, the juice of one lemon, 8 basil leaves and 10ozs of cooked baby shrimp.

Fill a saucepan with water, add salt and bring to the boil. Add half an ounce of olive oil and the noodles and cook for7 minutes, then drain. To prevent further cooking, run cold water over the noodles.

Peel the tomatoes by plunging them into boiling water for one minute. Cut them in half and squeeze each half to remove the seeds, then pureein a blender, season with salt and pepper, and with the motor still running, add the lemon juice and the rest of the olive oil. Then strain this puree through a fine sieve.

Drain the baby shrimp and squeeze them in a cheese cloth until they form a sauce. Chop four of the basic leaves and add to the sauce. Combine the fettucine with a bit of the sauce, and arrange on a serving dish or plate. Pour the remaining sauce over the noodles and garnish with the remaining basil leaves. Finally season to taste before serving.

Lobster Thermidor a la Bermuda

Ingredients
one lobster, salt and freshly ground black pepper, 1 oz oil, half a cup of butter, 2 tablespoons of flour, one cup of milk, 1 egg yolk, 2 tablespoons of heavy cream, 1 tablespoon of English mustard, half a cup of shredded Swiss cheese, half a cup of Hollandaise sauce.

Split the lobster in half lengthwise, season with salt and pepper and brush with a few drops of oil, then cook in a baking dish in a 400 degree oven for 15 minutes. Baste every 5 minutes with melted butter. When cooked, remove the meat from the tails and set aside.

Preparing the sauce: Make a roux with 2 tablespoons of butter and the flour, then gradually add the milk while stirring with a whisk. Season with salt and boil for one minute. Remove from heat and add the egg yolk which has been beaten with the cream. Add the mustard.

Chop the lobster meat coarsely and add it to most of the sauce, mix well and then fill the shells with the mixture. Sprinkle with the grated cheese and cover with a final layer of Hollandaise sauce.

Fillet of Wahoo with green peppercorns and Bermuda oranges

Ingredients
4 wahoo fillets (fresh tuna or similar), about six oz each (or similar fish), juice of 2 oranges, 2 Bermuda oranges, salt and freshly ground pepper, 6 tablespoons of butter, quarter of a cup of fish stock, two ozs Noilly Prat, 1 cup heavy cream and 8 small mint leaves.

Marinate the fillets for 1 to 2 hours in the orange juice, the zest of one orange and salt and pepper. Peel the 2 Bermuda oranges and divide into seg-ments. Melt 2 tablespoons of butter in a frying pan and add the marinted fillets. Add the fish stock, Noilly Prat and white wine, and cover and poach gently for 3 minutes on each side until fully cooked.

Remove the fish and keep warm. Reduce the cooking liquid until it has the consistency of marmalade, then add the green peppers and cream. Reduce for a further 5 minutes, then gradually add the remaining 4 tablespoons of butter. Season to taste and reheat the fillets in the sauce. Add the orange segments and garnish with mint leaves.

Stuffed Bermuda Bananas

Ingredients
Two ozs of raisins, 6 tablespoons of Bermuda black rum, six ozs of soft butter, two ozs icing sugar, two ozs heavy cream, two oz powdered milk, I teaspoon vanilla extract, 6 bananas, two oz unsalted peanuts, 12 glace cherries and whipped cream for decoration.

Soak the raisins in the rum for at least an hour. In a bowl combine the butter and icing sugar, and using a whisk, beat in the milk powder, cream and vanilla. Drain the raisins and fold them into the creamed mixture.

Cut the unpeeled bananas in half lengthwise and, being careful not to break the skins, separate the bananas from the skins and set the skins aside. Pour the lemon juice over the bananas and mash them with a fork, and add to the creamed mixture. Carefully fill the banana skins with the creamed mixture, sprinkle with crushed peanuts and decorate with whipped cream and slices of glace cherries. Keep refrigerated until ready to serve.

There are lots more island recipes in *Bermudian Cookery*, com-piled by the Bermuda Junior Service League, a women's volunteer organisation which sponsors and makes donations to a large num-ber of Bermudian charities and projects. The cookbook is available in bookshops, stores and hotels throughout the island.

2 ISLAND TOUR

• GETTING AROUND •

There is no car rental on Bermuda and visitors get around by using taxis, bus, ferries, scooters, bicycles or on foot. There are well over 100 miles (160km) of road which allow access to all parts of the island, but while most road surfaces are very good, some roads are narrow and twisting, with lots of blind bends and tight corners. The more off the beaten track you get, the more variable are the road surface and conditions are. Getting from one attraction to the next generally takes longer than expected, especially as you need to take time to stop and enjoy the views and take photos, or perhaps take a dip in the sea or get a drink or snack.

By Bus

There are regular scheduled bus services to most points around Bermuda, and bus stops are easily recognized by their little shelters or blue and pink striped poles.

The blue and pink buses have large windows so you can enjoy the view and it is a great way to get into conversation with locals and others visitors. Buses run from Hamilton along North Shore Road and Middle Road to the airport every 15

Useful tip

Poles that are blue on top indicate services outbound from Hamilton, while those poles with pink on top indicate buses heading to Hamilton. Buses do not allow passengers on with large pieces of luggage so you must take a taxi if heading to or from the airport or if you have bought a lot of shopping. All stops are request stops. If you are on the bus, press the buzzer to alert the driver that you want to get off at the next stop, and if you are waiting at a bus stop, stick out your arm.

minutes for most of the day. Buses do not run anywhere, however, late at night.

There are several bus routes and if you plan to use this form of very convenient and accessible transport a lot, pick up a bus and ferry schedule from the bus terminus or tourist office. The island is divided into 14 zones. Zone 1 includes St George's and areas and zones change every two miles or so until you reach the Royal Naval Dockyard which is Zone 13. Zone 14 takes in St David's, the airport, former US Naval Air Station and the Clearwater Beaches.

Adult fares: cash fares require exact change only. The cash fare for the journey up to 3 zones is $2.50, while longer journeys cost $4.00. Drivers cannot give change and passengers must have the exact fare or tokens. Dollar bills are not accepted. Tokens are available for 3 and 14 zones, and are useable on buses and ferries. Tickets for 3 and 14 zones are sold in booklets of 15, and are useable on buses only. Transportation Passes for 1, 3 or 7 consecutive days and Calendar Month Passes are available for an unlimited number of journeys for all zones, and may be used on buses and ferries.

Tokens, tickets and Transportation Passes are available from the PTB Central Terminal on Washington Street, Hamilton.

Tokens and Transportation Passes are also available from the Visitors Service Bureau and guest houses. The Central Terminal hours of operation are 7.15am-5.30pm Monday-Friday, 8.15am-5.30pm on Saturday and 9.15am-4.45pm on Sundays and holidays. Contact the Public Transportation Board at ☎ 292-3851 for additional information.

Passengers must have exact fare in coins, or use a token or ticket which can be bought in advance and offer substantial savings. Books of 15 tickets for 3 zone ($15) or 4 or more zone travel ($24), are sold at hotels, most sub Post Offices (but not the General Post Office) or the Central bus terminal in Washington Street, off Church Street and just east of City Hall, Hamilton. From Front Street and Reid Street you can get to the terminal via Walker Arcade and Washington Mall.

Mini Buses operate in St George's including Ferry Reach and St David's, and West End between Somerset Bridge and Watford Bridge to the Royal Naval Dockyard.

Continued on page 52...

Island sightseeing and self-guided tours

The roads of Bermuda are still officially known as the carriageways, a reminder of the recent past when the horse and carriage was the main method of transportation. Today, the horse and carriage is still an important island institution, and traditionally used to convey brides to church. It is also a great way to take an island tour and for a touch of romance, take an evening moonlit ride.

Taxis

A full day's hire is calculated as six consecutive daylight hours. Special all inclusive pre-sold tours are available and qualified 'Blue Flag' taxi tour guides are available for island and specialist trips.

Buses

These run to schedule and are a reliable and economical way to get around so it is possible to work out your own tour by bus hopping from the one attraction to another. You can even combine bus and ferries by using the Bus and Ferry Schedule. A suggested day out could be:

10.00am	Leave Hamilton on the 'Dockyard' bus and enjoy views along the South Shore.
11.05am	Arrive at the Dockyard and Maritime Museum.
12.35pm	Leave Dockyard on 'Hamilton' bus.

12.45pm	Alight at Mangrove Bay for waterside lunch and shopping.
14.55pm	Leave Watford Bridge by ferry via Cavello Bridge and Somerset Bridge for Hamilton.
15.45pm	Land at Hamilton Ferry Terminal.

Boat tours

There are swimming, fishing, snorkeling, sightseeing and just sun and relaxation tours aboard piloted ketches, sloops, yals, powerful catamarans or lavish, air conditioned cruisers. You can sightsee during the day, watch the sunset and enjoy a romantic dinner afloat.

Glass Bottom Boat Tours offer the chance to view some of the 200 sq miles (520 sq km) of coral reefs and 350 wrecks which surround the island. There are day and night tours and both are worth taking because they offer very different views of this constantly changing undersea world.

Submarine Tours

Enterprise Submarine operates from Sunday to Thursday between May and November and tenders leave from Hamilton and the Royal Naval Dockyard between 9am and 5pm. Reservations are required ☎ 234-3547.

Helicopter Tours

Bermuda Helicopters operate tours daily between 8am and 6pm April to October. Advance booking is required ☎ 295-1180/293-4800.

Route 1: Hamilton to Grotto Bay (47 minutes) and St George's (65 minutes) via Marriott's Castle and The Caves.

Route 2: Hamilton to the Ord Road (25 minutes) via the Botanical Gardens and Elbow Beach.

Route 3: Hamilton to Grotto Bay (40 minutes) and St George's (58 minutes) via Middle Road and The Caves.

Route 4: Hamilton to Spanish Point (12 minutes) via St John's Road.

Route 5: Hamilton to Pond Hill (10 minutes) via Parson's Road and Glebe Road.

Route 6: St George's to St David's (25 minutes) via the USNAS Main Gate Route 7 Hamilton to the Royal Naval Dockyard (62 minutes) via Barnes Corner and the South Shore Beaches.

Route 8: Hamilton to the Dockyard (62 minutes) and Somerset via Middle Road, Cedar Hill (23 minutes) and Barnes Corner (34 minutes).

Route 9: Hamilton to Prospect (10 minutes).

Route 10: Hamilton to St George's (50 minutes) via Palmetto Road, Aquarium and Perfume Factory.

Route 11: Hamilton to St George's (50 minutes) via North Shore, Blackwatch Pass and Aquarium.

Ferries

In 1902 Walter Ingham ferried passengers in his rowboat around the Harbour. By the time he arrived in 1952, he had rowed the equivalent of eight times around the world. Today, the diesel powered ferries are an economic and convenient way to travel around the West End. Passengers to West End can even take their scooters with them for a charge and ride back, while bicycles are carried free. The ferry terminal is next to the Visitors Service Bureau on Front Street, Hamilton. There are ferries between Hamilton Harbour and Paget, Warwick, Somerset and Dockyard.

Ferries from Hamilton to the Paget area run from 7.15am Monday to Friday and 8.50am on Saturday, and call at Lower Ferry, Hodson's and Salt Kettle before returning to Hamilton. The round trip takes 25 minutes. The last ferry leaves Hamilton by 11pm and returns to the capital at 11.30pm. On

Sunday the first ferry leaves Hamilton at 10.10am and the last sails at 7pm.

Warwick Ferry

The first Warwick area ferry leaves Hamilton at 7.15 on Monday to Friday and 8.45am on Saturday, and calls at Darrell's and Belmont before returning to Hamilton. The round trip takes 25 minutes and the last ferry leaves Hamilton 11am returning at 11.30pm. On Sunday the first ferry leaves Hamilton at 10.10am and the last sails at 7pm.

Hamilton Ferry

The first Hamilton to Somerset and Dockyard ferry leaves the capital at 6.25am Monday to Friday and 9am on Saturday. It calls at the Dockyard, Boaz Island, Watford Bridge, Cavello Bay and Somerset Bridge before returning to Hamilton. The round trip takes 1 hour and 45 minutes. The last ferry leaves Hamilton at 5.20pm and returns to the capital landing at 7.05pm. On Sunday the first ferry leaves Hamilton at 9am and the last one at 5pm.

Note: Bus and ferry passengers should take advantage of the Transportation Pass, which is available for one, three or seven days and offers unlimited use during that period of all buses and ferries. The pass is sold at the Central Terminal, Visitors Service Bureau in Hamilton, some hotels and guest houses, and at other signposted authorized outlets.

Taxis

These can be hired by the meter, hour or day. All taxis are metered with the tariffs fixed by law, and the rates per cab are the same for one person up to a maximum of six. There is a surcharge for travel between midnight and 7 am, on Sundays and for extra large pieces of luggage.

Handy tip: Taxis displaying a blue pennant indicate the driver is a qualified tour guide.

Horse drawn carriages can be hired for half an hour and longer by agreement. Expect to pay $25-$30 for half an hour for one to four passengers. A list of fares should be on display.

Scooters and mopeds (motor assisted cycles)

No driving license is required but you must be 16 or over to drive either a scooter or moped, and safety helmets are required by law for both drivers and passengers. When you rent the scooter you will be given a lock which you should use when not riding it.

Bermuda Railway and Railway Trail

Affectionately known as 'Old Rattle and Shake', it opened on 31 October, 1931 and was sold to British Guiana lock, stock and barrel after the Second World War when cars were introduced. The Railway Trail now follows 18 miles (29km) of the former track and is divided into seven separate walks which run the length of the island. Three miles of the original route were used to create roads in and around Hamilton, so do not appear on the Railway Trail. The walks vary in length from just under 2 miles (3km) to just over 3 miles (5km), and are detailed in the excellent and illustrated Bermuda Railway Trail Guide leaflet which is available from tourist offices. Remember that if you are on foot and are not being picked up you will have to walk back to your starting point or catch a bus if there is a convenient stop. The trail runs from Somerset Station at the western end of the island to Ferry Point Park on St George's, and there are many trails running from it to island attractions, historic sights, natures reserves and beaches. You can walk the trail, travel by bicycle or moped or ride on horseback. It is best to walk with a companion or in groups.

The idea for the railway was first mentioned in plans in 1899 but it was not until 1922 that the Bermuda Parliament gave the go ahead and work started with initial private financing of £100,000. Because landowners were reluctant to give up their land, the engineers planned the route to hug the shoreline as much as possible. In fact, one tenth of the 21 miles (28km) route was carried on 38 trestle bridges, 16 of which crossed over water. The piers of the original bridges can still be seen around the island. By the time the railway opened in 1931 the cost had soared to more than £1 million making it

Above: Remains of old railway bridge, Baileys Bay
Below: Explore the Railway trail

the most costly railway, mile for mile, ever built anywhere. At a construction rate of just two and a half miles (4km) a year, it was also the slowest. It was a grand railway, however, with individual wicker chairs for the first class passengers, bench seats in second class and a large goods van which took bicycles. During the Second World War the railway carried both islanders and the many military personnel based on the island but because of the difficulty of getting replacements, the rolling stock and permanent way deteriorated. In 1946 the railway was faced with bankruptcy and was bailed out by the Government which bought it for £150,000. The estimated cost of putting things right was in excess of £1 million and the Government decided it was better to sell the railway to British Guiana, now Guyana. At the same time, private motor cars were allowed so the passing of the railway was not as traumatic as it might otherwise have been. In 17 years, the railway carried 14 million passengers, and today it still provides a popular and scenic byway for visitors and locals alike to enjoy.

Section One

1.75 miles (3 km), 1.5 hours, suitable for cycling and scooters.

It starts from the Somerset Bus Terminal, the original terminus station and runs past the Springfield Plantation House and Gilbert Nature Reserve, past Harmon's Bay, the Heydon Trust estate and Fort Scaur to Somerset Bridge where you can be picked up, catch a bus or take the ferry.

Section Two

2.25 miles (3.5 km), 2 hours, suitable for cycles and in some sections for scooters.

It starts at Somerset Bridge and takes in Overplus Lane, Evans Pond, the former Evans Bay Station now a Sunday School, Franks Bay and ends at Middle Road.

Section Three

3.25 miles (5 km), 3 hours, no scooters allowed.

It starts from Middle Road and takes in Black Bay with detours to Gibbs Hill lighthouse, passes Jews Bay and the Southampton Princess Resort, South Shore Beach Parklands, Khyber Pass quarry and ends close to the Warwick Pond bird sanctuary.

Section Four

2.25 miles (3.5km), 2 hours, no scooters.

It starts on Dunscombe Road close to Belmont Golf Course, and takes in many fine old homes and woodlands with superb views of Hamilton over Great Sound. It passes Paget Marsh and ends at the old Railway Tunnel which ran for 450 feet (137m) under South Road.

Section Five

1.25 miles (2 km), 1.5 hours, no scooters.

It starts at Palmetto Park on the north coast, passes Palmetto House, Penhurst Park and Gibbet Island – where witches were burned and criminals hanged – and runs to Flatts Inlet, a short walk from Flatts Village.

Section Six

3.5 miles (6 km), 3 hours, no scooters.

The walk starts at Coney Island and passes Bailey's Bay and Shelly Bay Park to Aquarium Station.

Section Seven

2.75 miles (4.5 km), 2.5 hours, no scooters.

It starts at the old St George's Terminal in Tiger Bay Gardens and passes Mullet Bay Park, Rocky Hill Park, Sugarloaf Hill, Lover's Lake Nature Reserve, a 100 year-old lime kiln and ends at Ferry Point Park.

• HAMILTON •

Hamilton, named after Governor Henry Hamilton (1788-94) is one of the world's smallest, busiest ports, and has been the island capital since January, 1815. It is a charming compact town with its busy waterfront, historic buildings, museums and galleries and surrounded by pastel shaded cottages and their pretty gardens. It is the administrative heart of the island with government buildings and law courts, and also the main shopping complex with large stores and unique boutiques. Front Street boasts its restaurants and waterside bars and traditional English-style pubs. The ferry terminal and main bus station, both a short walk away, offer easy travel to all parts of the island. The heart of the town is easy to explore on foot and most of the sights, museums, galleries and historic buildings are contained within a few blocks of the waterfront.

A Bermudian 'Bobby' conducts traffic in Hamilton

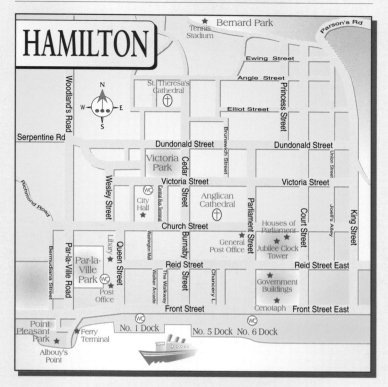

A walking tour

Start at the **Tourist Visitors Centre** in the **Ferry Terminal** in Front Street. You can pick up brochures and maps and find out about the latest events and attractions. Pretty Front Street is Hamilton's main thoroughfare running along the water's edge, and it is busy day and night, with its stores and boutiques attracting shoppers during the day, and its restaurants, bars and pubs drawing diners and those looking for nightlife. Many of the buildings have balconies from which you can enjoy a drink and watch the world go by.

The street which is usually packed with people, taxis, mopeds and scooters, used to have railroad tracks running along which carried the Bermuda Railway in the 1930s and early 1940s.

The ferry terminal is the departure point for boats crossing the Great Sound to Paget,

59

Warwick, Somerset, Sandys and the Dockyard, and alongside are the quays where tour boats and glass bottom boats leave for the Sea Gardens off Daniel's Head on Somerset Island. Often the glass bottom boats are dwarfed as they lie moored under the bows of the huge cruise ships. On most days through the summer you can see cruise ships moored either alongside the pink passenger terminal No 1 Shed, or the other two terminals further east along Front Street. During the winter, No 1 Shed is the venue for the **Gombey Review** which takes place at 3pm on Tuesdays. The highly decorative masks and costumes are thought to have been introduced to the island from Angola in the 17th century. The drumming and dancing was traditionally confined to the New Year, but the exhuberant displays now feature year round in parades and special events.

Bermuda Chamber of Commerce

Behind the ferry terminal is the **Bermuda Chamber of Commerce** which is dwarfed by the headquarters of the **Bank of Bermuda**. In the building's mezzanine you can view the Coin Exhibition which contains a fascinating collection of ancient coins including the island's first currency known as hogge money. It is claimed that when the *Sea Venture* foundered in 1609 and the survivors struggled ashore the only animals they could see were wild pigs. In 1616 when the Bermuda Company issued its first money, the coins carried an imprint of the *Sea Venture* on one side, and a wild hog on the other. The exhibition is open to the public from Monday to Thursday between 9.30am and 3pm and on Friday from 9.30am to 4.30pm. Admission is free ☎ 295-4000.

Point Pleasant Road runs down to **Albuoy's Point** which is now a waterfront park with some trees for shade and benches where you can see and watch the Harbour activity. To the west is the small waterside **Barr's Bay Park** which looks out over Barr's Bay and the **Royal Bermuda Yacht Club**. The club was granted its Royal accolade by Prince Albert in 1845, and today it hosts some of the premier events in the yachting world's calendar.

Inland from the Visitor Centre at the junction of Queen Street and Front Street is the **Birdcage**, which is named after its designer Michael 'Dickey' Bird. It was erected for the police so that they could conduct the traffic at the busy intersection, and is still used on occasions. The junction itself is known as **Heyl's Corner** after a 19th century apothecary who had a shop there.

Queen Street

Queen Street is the home of the Bermuda Book Store, and the historic white two-floor, shuttered historic **Perot Post Office** which was built in the early 1840s as a post office and still operates as one today.

Church Street

Turn right into Church Street and on your left is the white **City Hall**, designed by Wilfred Onions, and home of the **Civic Centre and Theatre**, the Bermuda **National Gallery** and the Bermuda Society of Arts Gallery. It is set back from the road behind a lawn, fountains and a small lake. Look up at the weather vane on the roof which shows the *Sea Venture*. The building was opened in 1960 and after passing through the huge cedar doors into the chandeliered lobby, you can visit the portrait gallery with pictures of former mayors of Hamilton. Also on display is the Coin and Note Collection of the Bermuda Monetary Authority and the Benbow Stamp Collection. City Hall is open from Monday to Friday between 9am and 5pm and admission is free ☎ 292-1234.

The **Bermuda National Gallery**, which opened in 1992 with a temperature and humidity controlled interior, contains the permanent Watlington Collection which includes works by Renaissance and Old Master painters such as Gainsborough, Romney and Reynolds as well as contemporary works. There are also a number of fascinating old paintings depicting life and scenes on Bermuda painted by Winslow Homer, Georgia O'Keeffe, Charles Demuth and others. The gallery also hosts visiting exhibitions. The gallery is open Monday to Saturday from 10am to 4pm and from 12.30pm to 4pm on Sunday ☎ 295-9428.

The **Bermuda Society of Arts Gallery** features regular shows by local artists, sculptors and photographers, as well as staging special events, one man shows and travelling exhibitions. It is open Monday to Friday from 10am to 4pm and on Saturday from 9am to noon ☎ 292-3824.

Continue along Church Street then turn left into

Continued on page 64...

William Perot

William Perot, Bermuda's first post master, who used to hand stamp all letters. His friend J. B. Heyl, the apothecarist, is credited with the idea of selling books of stamps so that people sending mail could stick on their own stamps. The first Perot stamps appeared in 1848 and these early stamps are now extremely rare and very valuable. A world record was set in June, 1991 when an 1854 Perot Postmaster's one penny red stamp attached to a letter was sold at auction in London for £203,500 ($350,000). The post office still displays a portrait of Queen Victoria as well as Perot family members, and is open from Monday to Saturday between 9am and 5pm ☎ 925-5151.

Behind is **Par-La-Ville Park** which provides a lush oasis of green and calm. It is a popular spot with workers enjoying an open air lunchbreak, and it was one of Perot's favorite places. It is claimed that Perot much preferred to spend his time in the gardens rather than collecting and stamping the mail, and it was this that persuaded him to adopt Heyl's idea and produce the stamps. It also boasts a famous Moon Gate, the round stone gate which is a Bermudian feature and supposed to bring good luck to all who pass through. After being married, couples will usually walk hand in hand through a moon gate to ensure a long and happy marriage.

Next to the post office is Perot's former home and now the **Library** and **Museum of the Bermuda Historical Society**. Founded in 1843 the library is one of the oldest in the Western Hemisphere and it moved to its present location in 1916. The reference section contains a priceless collection of old books about the island, and there are newspaper cuttings dating back to 1784 on microfilm. Lending facilities are extended to visitors for a nominal fee. The library is open from 9.30am to 6pm Monday to Friday and from 9.30am to 5pm on Saturday ☎ 295-2905. The museum's entrance hall is graced by portraits of Sir George Somers and his wife while portraits of Perot and his wife are displayed inside. Exhibits include early Somers memorabilia, ancient books and charts, Bermuda silver, and many unusual items that found their way to the island brought by ships which sailed around the world. A prize exhibit is a letter written by George Washington in 1775 to the people of Bermuda asking for gunpowder. The museum is open from Monday to Saturday between 9.30am and 3.30pm, and the Library is open Monday to Friday from 9.30am to 6pm and on Saturday from 9.30am to 5pm. Admission is free ☎ 295-2487.

The giant rubber tree in front of the building is said to have been planted by Perot and was commented on by Mark Twain on one of his frequent visits to the island.

Above: Hamilton's neo-gothic Anglican Cathedral
Below: The busy Front Street, Hamilton

Washington Street to its junction with Victoria Street. Opposite is **Victoria Park,** opened in 1890 to commemorate the Golden Jubilee of Queen Victoria. The 4 acre (1.6 hectare) park has a sunken garden and Victorian Grandstand. It is open daily from 8 am to sunset.

Continue east on Victoria Street then left on Cedar Avenue to its junction with Elliot Street and the Spanish mission style **St Theresa's Roman Catholic Cathedral.** Built in 1932, the church has a gold and silver chalice which was presented by Pope Paul VI when he visited in 1968. It is open daily and admission is free ☎ 292-0607.

Head back down Cedar Avenue and Burnaby Street, then left into Church Street and the **Cathedral of the Most Holy Trinity.** The Anglican cathedral was consecrated in 1911 on the site of a church built in 1872 and believed to have been deliberately burned to the ground in 1884. Work started on the present Gothic church in 1885 but took 26 years to complete. Materials for the church were imported from around the world. Scottish granite supports the clerestory in the nave, the altar in the Lady Chapel is of Italian marble, the choir pews are carved from English oak and the main structure is built in Bermuda limestone. The

Warrior Chapel is dedicated to islanders who died serving their country, and the Great Warrior Window was installed to commemorate Bermudian men who died during the First World War. You can climb the steps to the top of the 145 foot (44m) high tower for sensational views. The cathedral and tower are open daily from 8 am to 4.45 pm. There is a charge to scale the tower ☎ 292-4033. A little further along Church Street is St Andrew's Presbyterian Church, founded in 1843, and the oldest in the city. It is open Monday to Thursday from 9 am to noon.

Parliament Street

Continue east past the **General Post Office** and turn right into Parliament Street. On your left is the Italianate **Sessions House,** home of the Supreme Court and House of Assembly.

The **Bermuda Archives** are down the road at 30 Parliament Street, and are open from Monday to Friday between 8.45 am and 5 pm. Admission is free ☎ 295-5151.

Continue south on Parliament Street to Reid Street and the **Cabinet Building.** It is set in impressive grounds with flower beds, manicured lawns and stately trees, and houses the offices of the Prime Minister and Senate, the legislature's upper house. It is the venue for

The Sessions House

The original building was built in two-floors in 1819, and much of the embellishment such as the clock tower and colonnade were added in 1887 to celebrate Queen Victoria's Golden Jubilee. The Victoria Jubilee clock tower was opened at midnight on the last day of 1893 so that its first act could be to chime out the old year and bring in the new.

The House of Assembly, the legislature's lower house, meets on the second floor with all the pomp and pageantry of the Mother Parliament in Westminster, with bewigged and robed Speaker and mace bearing Sergeant-at-Arms. The mace was presented to the Sessions House in 1921 and is a replica of the James I mace in the Crown Jewel Collection in the Tower of London. The gavel used by the Speaker is said to have been made from a cedar bough taken from an ancient tree in St Peter's Churchyard, St George. The tree was growing in 1620 when the island's first parliament met in St George's. The Supreme Court proceedings are equally impressive, especially the official opening of the law terms when the judges parade in all their regalia.

The Sessions House is open from Monday to Friday from 9am to 5pm ☎ 292-7408.

the impressive and formal Opening of Parliament which takes place on the first Friday in November and is attended by the Governor, Speaker of the House, members of the Senate and Representatives. The Governor's speech contains proposed legislation for the coming year and is delivered from the 'throne', made from cedar and bearing the carved inscription 'Cap Josias Forstore Governor of the Sumer Islands Anodo 1642' (Josias Forstore was Governor of Bermuda in 1642) and overlooked by paintings of King George III and Queen Charlotte. It is open Monday to Friday from 9am to 5pm and admission is free, even when the Senate is sitting on Wednesdays ☎ 292-5501.

Opposite in Parliament Street is the **Police Station**. Continue along Reid Street left into King Street and then past the Fire Station and right into Happy Valley Road for the entrance to **Fort Hamilton**.

Fort Hamilton

The fort is on the outskirts of the city and a fairly long walk, so you may want to leave it to another day or take a taxi there. The fort was built on the orders of the Duke of Wellington and was surrounded by a moat, which is now planted as a small and very pretty botanical garden. The fort, protected by huge 18 ton cannon, never fired a shot in anger. It now offers spectacular views and is an interesting place to explore because of its many underground tunnels which were carved out of solid rock by Royal Engineers sappers in the 1870s. It still has an impressive array of armaments and the views from the ramparts over Hamilton and the Harbour are splendid.

At noon every Monday from November to March, the Bermuda Isles Highland Pipe Band in full tartan perform the Skirling Ceremony on the green with pipers, drummers and dancers. The fort is open Monday to Friday from 9.30am to 5pm.

The Sessions House, Bermuda's House of Parliament

Front Street

Head back to King Street and walk down to the waterfront and then return west along Front Street past the grounds of the Cabinet Buildings and the **Cenotaph** which is modeled on the one in Whitehall in London. The foundation stone was laid in 1920 by the Prince of Wales, later Edward VIII who abdicated in 1936 to marry American divorcee Mrs Simpson.

Almost every shop and boutique along Front Street is worth visiting, but if you are interested in art, take in **The Gallery** in The Emporium, 69 Front Street, which features work by local artists. It is open from Monday to Saturday between 10am and 4,30 pm ☎ 295-8980. The **Masterworks Foundation,** 41 Front Street, also has art exhibits and shows.

It is open from 10am to 4pm Monday to Saturday ☎ 295-5580.

It is then a short walk back to the ferry terminal and the Tourist Visitor's Centre.

TOURING THE ISLAND

Parishes

Bermuda is divided into 9 parishes which run from St George's in the east, through to Hamilton, Smith's, Devonshire, Pembroke, Paget, Warwick and Southampton to Sandys at the west end. The parishes, with the exception of St George's are based on the original 'tribes' (shares of land) drawn by Richard Norwood in 1615 when he produced the first definitive map of Bermuda. Each tribe was named after an investor in the Bermuda Company. As St George's was the original capital the surrounding land was used for grazing and considered public land.

The parishes are still important and if you ask an islander for directions, you are likely to be told that the place you want is in Paget or Smith's as a general locator.

You will also see the original Tribe Roads which tend to run north to south, especially in the western half of the island. The three main settlements are Hamilton, St

George's and Somerset Village in Sandys.

The main island routes are the North Shore Road, South Shore Road and Middle Road which runs through the middle of the island, and Harbour Road which runs along the southern shores of Great Sound. From these main roads are scores of secondary roads and country lanes which used to feed old plantations and farmsteads.

The island is easy to explore but take your time. There should be no need to rush and it makes sense to divide Bermuda into three tour areas, east, central and west.

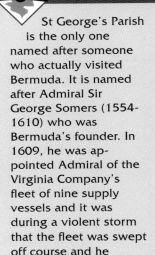

St George's Parish is the only one named after someone who actually visited Bermuda. It is named after Admiral Sir George Somers (1554-1610) who was Bermuda's founder. In 1609, he was appointed Admiral of the Virginia Company's fleet of nine supply vessels and it was during a violent storm that the fleet was swept off course and he arrived in Bermuda.

The other parishes are:

Devonshire – named after William Cavendish, Ist Earl of Devonshire (1552-1626). He invested heavily in the island but never visited.

Hamilton – named after James, 2nd Marquis of Hamilton (1589-1625). He was a staunch supporter of King James and was appointed a

Parish names –their origins

Member of the Council for the Plantations but he never visited Bermuda or the New World colonies.

Paget – named after William, 4th Lord Paget (1572-1629). He was a member of the Virginia Company which controlled Bermuda but never visited the island.

Pembroke – named after the 3rd Earl of Pembroke (1580-1630) a nephew of Sir Philip Sydney, the richest nobleman in Britain. He was a great patron of the arts and Shakespeare dedicated his first folio printing to him. He never visited Bermuda.

Sandys – named after Sir Edwin Sandys (1561-1629), the second son of the Archbishop of York. He was a member of the Council for Virginia in 1607 and joined the Bermuda Company in 1615 but never visited.

Smith's – named after Sir Thomas Smith (1588-1625) a self-made millionaire. He started work as a haberdasher's assistant but through his business skills accumulated a massive fortune. He was appointed the first Governor of the East India Company and invested heavily in Bermuda, but never visited.

Southampton – named after Henry Wriothesley, the 3rd Earl of Southampton. (1573-1624). Another patron of the arts, especially Shakespeare who dedicated some of his sonnets to him. While he invested heavily in Bermuda and the America, he never visited.

Warwick – named after Robert, 2nd Earl of Warwick (1587-1638). He was appointed a member of the Bermuda Company but declined to visit.

TOUR 1 – CENTRAL BERMUDA
Pembroke, Devonshire and Smith's Parishes

From Hamilton follow the shoreline west and then take Bay Road which runs across the island to **Deep Bay, Admiralty House Park** and **Clarence Cove**. The land was owned by John Dunscombe who later became Lieutentant Governor of Newfoundland, and he sold it in 1816 to the Royal Navy who wanted to build a house for the Admiral in charge of the Dockyard. Several houses were built on the site and it was occupied until 1951 when the Royal Navy left the island. The house was then demolished and all that remains is the ballroom. The grounds run down to the coast and there are many caves in the surrounding cliffs as well as sheltered coves. One of these is the man-made Admiral's Cave. Close to Admiralty House Park is the entrance to a tunnel said to have been built by English convicts transported to the island. It is said that the Admiral wanted the tunnel built so that he could have discreet assignations with a lady friend.

The road then turns left on to Spanish Point Road for **Spanish Point** which stands at the end of the peninsula, and is believed to be the point where Diego Ramirez landed a handful of years before the survivors of the *Sea Venture* came ashore. There is a small park around the sheltered beach which is suitable for swimming and picnics. It is a popular area during the summer with campers. There are good views across the water to the Royal Naval Dockyard. **Cobbler's Island** lies just off the point and it is said that runaway slaves were executed here and their bodies displayed as a deterrent to others.

Government House

Retrace your route to Deep Bay and then continue along North Shore Road. The road passes **Langton Hill** and **Government House** which looks out over the ocean. The house has been the official residence of the Governor since the capital moved to Hamilton in 1815, although the original building was replaced by the present structure in 1892. The house is set in extensive landscaped grounds but is not open to the public. Over the years, however, it has played host to numerous famous people from Winston Churchill and Presidents Kennedy and Bush to almost all the current senior members of the Royal Family.

Above: Verdmont Historic Manor House
Below: Mangrove Bay & Marina

Langton Hill connects with St John's Road and **St John's Church**, the parish church for Pembroke. The present church was consecrated in 1826 and stands on the site of a church built in 1621. The churchyard was the scene of a remarkable dispute in 1874 during the funeral of Esther Levy. A Weslyan Minister appeared in the churchyard saying that he had been asked by Esther's relatives to conduct the service. The Anglican vicar insisted the Weslyan minister had no authority to conduct the service within the churchyard, and eventually the vicar accused the Weslyan of trespassing. The case went all the way to the Supreme Court with the vicar getting judgment and the Weslyan minister fined one shilling. The church, which has one of the finest organs on the island, is open daily from 8am to 5.30pm and admission is free ☎ 292-0299.

After a short distance you pass the entrance to the impressive **Black Watch Pass** on your right, which was literally carved out of the limestone rock, and **Black Watch Well**. The well was dug by soldiers of the Scottish Black Watch regiment during a drought in 1849. Almost opposite the well is Ducking Stool Park where miscreants were punished in the 17th and 18th centuries.

Inland there is **Pembroke Marsh** while the North Shore Road runs to **Devonshire Dock** where local fishermen land their catches which can be bought fresh. During the 1812 war, Royal Navy ships anchored offshore to take on supplies, water and new crews.

You then pass **Robinson's Bay** and **Palmetto Park.** You can visit **Palmetto House** which is on your right just past the next roundabout. It is an early 18th century cruciform house now owned by the Bermuda National Trust with 3 main rooms on view with fine period furniture. It is open on Thursday from 10am to 5pm and admission is free ☎ 295-9941.

Continue along North Shore Road past **Penshurst Park,** a public park, until you arrive at **Flatt's Inlet** with **Gibbet Island** just offshore. The island gets its name because it was where public executions were carried out by hanging. Witches were also burned at the stake here.

You can cross over Flatt's Bridge – the boundary between Smith's and Hamilton parishes – and continue to St George's while our route takes us down the western shores of Harrington Sound on Harrington Sound Road.

At **Bronson Hartley's Underwater Wonderland** you can explore the coral reefs even if you have no scuba or snorkeling experience. You use helmets, a bit like old deep sea divers, to walk along the sea bed 10-12 feet (3-3.6m) below the surface.

The road then continues south beside Harrington Sound to **Devil's Hole Hill** and the **Devil's Hole Aquarium** on Harrington Sound Road. The aquarium claims the title as the island's first tourist attraction although this came about more by accident than design. A member of the Trott family built a fish pond in 1830 and put a protective wall around it. So many people asked him what was on the other side that he started to charge people to take a look. The aquarium is really a deep pool which has a large range of fish and marine creatures, including sharks and turtles. It is open daily from 8am to 6pm during the summer and from 10am to 5pm between Nov and March. There is an admission charge ☎ 293-2072.

South Road continues to **John Smith's Bay**, which is named after the 17th century adventurer Captain John Smith of Pocahontas fame. He was one of the founders of the Jamestown settlement in Virginia and in 1607 was ambushed by Indians. Indian chief Wahunsonacock ordered that Smith be killed but he was saved when Pocahontas, the chief's 13 year old daughter threw herself between him and the executioners. Smith later became President of the colony and a prolific writer and cartographer and traveled widely through the region visiting Bermuda many times. One of his many books was 'The Generall Historie of Virginia, New England and the Summer Isles'. The bay is great for swimming and snorkeling with a lifeguard on duty in the summer when a lunch wagon also calls.

Spittal Pond Nature Reserve

The road then passes **Gravelly Bay** to arrive at **Spittal Pond**, Bermuda's largest nature reserve. It covers 60 acres (24 hectares) and the home of two of the islands' unsolved mysteries. At the end of the winding trail that leads to Spanish Rock there is a bronze plaque bearing the inscription 'TF 1543'. It is claimed that the original inscription was carved in the rock itself by Theodore Fernando Camelo who landed in 1543 after being granted the islands by the Spanish crown. The rock was removed by the authorities and replaced by the plaque. Close by and high above on a cliff ledge overlooking the ocean, a checker board has been etched in the rock, although nobody knows how it got there or why. The waters are a refuge for a wide range of waders, ducks and sea birds, both resident and migratory, including the graceful Bermuda Longtail. November to March are the best times for birdwatchers. It is open daily from dawn to dusk and admission is free.

Continue past **Collector's Hill** named after Gilbert Salton, a revenue collector in the 19th century who lived nearby. It is said that he used to monitor the comings and goings of ships from his vantage point on top of the hill. He must have been fit because it is a fairly steep climb.

The **Verdmont Museum**, which dates from the late 17th century, stands on the top of the hill and the house is architecturally unique and historically fascinating. It is thought to have been built by John Dickinson, a ship owner about 1710. The three-floor Georgian mansion with its high chimneys and fireplaces in every room, was later the home of the eccentric privateer Captain Sayle, and John Green, an American loyalist who married one of Dickinson's grand daughters. He was a Judge in the Court of the Vice Admiralty and a talented painter and some of his family portraits still hang in the house. It also contains antiques many made from island cedar and mahogany, Georgian silver, and fine china and porcelain, plus a charming toy-filled nursery. A china coffee service is displayed which is said to have been a gift from Napoleon to US President Madison. The ship carrying it was seized by Capt Sayle and its contents commandeered. The museum which is operated by the Bermuda National Trust opened in 1956. Today it is open from Monday to Saturday between 9.30am and 4.30pm April to October, and 10am to 4pm November to March. There is a small admission charge ☎ 236-7369.

There is safe bathing on the fine beach at **Devonshire Bay** in a sheltered cove with lots of rock pools to explore. In the mid 19th century a huge gun battery was built beside the bay, one of the many fortifications ringing the island.

Inland there is the **Palm Grove Garden**, an 18 acre (7 hectare) private estate of manicured gardens, with hundreds of majestic palms and statues around a lake. The garden is open from Monday to Thursday from 9am to 5pm and admission is free. There is no telephone.

You can then cut inland on Brighton Hill Road to Middle Road to visit the **Old Devonshire Church**. The first church was built on the site in 1612 and was replaced in 1716. The second church was virtually raised to the ground after an explosion on Easter Sunday, 1970 and the current delightful stone and cedar building is a near exact reconstruction. Some parts of the church, notably the pews and three tier pulpit are said to be from the 1716 church, while some of the ecclesiastical silver dates from

1590 and was probably used in the 1612 church. It is open daily and admission is free ☎ 236-3671.

Stay on Middle Road heading west for the government-owned **Montpelier Arboretum** which has a wide variety of island plants and trees. It is open daily. A short drive then takes you back into Hamilton.

TOUR 2 – EAST BERMUDA
Hamilton, St George's and Tucker's Town

The tour starts at Flatt's Bridge and you take North Shore Road the short distance north to the **Bermuda Aquarium, Natural History Museum and Zoo** in Flatts Village alongside Harrington Sound. The bus from Hamilton stops right outside. The facility is an internationally recognized center for the preservation and re-introduction of threatened species, and includes more than 100 species of fish which can be found around Bermuda, from tiny darting wrasses and Sergeant Majors to giant moray eels and sharks. The aquarium, which opened in 1928, has a self guiding audio tour available to entertain and inform as you move from tank to tank. You can also meet Charlotte and Archie, the resident Californian Harbour Seals. The Natural History Museum explains about the island's beginnings, and has displays about the whaling industry, underseas exploration and the fragile environment both on land and below the water. In 1934 Dr William Beebe set a new record for a deep sea dive when his bathysphere descended more than half a mile (0.8km) off Bermuda. Outside there is the reptile walkway, primate enclosure, open aviary and new invertebrate house with its touch tank. It is open daily from 9am to 5pm and there is an admission charge ☎ 293-2727.

Close by is the **Bermuda Railway Museum**, 37 North Shore Road. The small museum is housed in the former Aquarium Station and is packed with railway memorabilia, including old photos and film, and gift shop. It is open Monday to Friday from 10am to 4pm and some Saturdays. Admission is free but donations are welcome ☎ 293-1774.

North Shore Road then follows the northern coast past **Shelly Bay** Beach, named after Henry Shelley one of the original settlers. He is said to have waded ashore here and he later wrote in his diary that the waters teemed with 'mullet and pilchards'. You can still wade out in the waist high water and watch the fishes swim around you. There is a children's playground and part of the area is now a protected nature reserve.

The road then cuts inland round **Crawl Hill** to **Crawl Point**. Crawl is a derivation of the Dutch word for a corral. Although corrals usually meant cattle enclosures, on Bermuda and throughout the Caribbean the expression was used to describe ponds usually surrounded by stones in which turtles could be kept until they were needed to eat.

A little further on is **Bailey's Bay** with Bay Island about 500 yards (457m) offshore. There are two beautiful beaches on the southwestern corner of the island which are only accessible at low tide. You have to swim out to the island and you should have some footwear because of the rocks as you come ashore. Shortly after the bay, there is a turning on the right into Trinity Church Road and **Holy Trinity Church** which dates from 1623 and overlooks Church Bay on Harrington Sound. The church originally had a thatched roof and while the core of that building remains it has been much added to and extended over the centuries. It has a very pretty small churchyard. The church is not generally open to the public

The Bermuda Perfumery

Head back to North Shore Road and the **Bermuda Perfumery**, 212 North Shore Road, which has been producing scents from blossoms, such as Easter lilies, frangipani, oleander, jasmine and passion flower, gathered in the lovely gardens around the 250 year cottage since 1935. You can tour the terraced gardens and trails, and learn how the perfumes are made using the ancient enfleurage process. It is open from Monday to Saturday between 9am and 5pm, and on Sunday from 9am to 4.30pm. Admission is free ☎ 293-0627.

but visitors are welcome to attend Sunday services.

The road then passes the **Wilkinson Memorial Park** before crossing into St George's Parish. The Coney Island Road follows the north coast to **Coney Island** and **Whale Bone Bay** but our route goes to **Blue Hole Hill.** This is a delightful area for walking and birdwatching with lots of large ponds. You can also swim in the sea at low tide but avoid areas of sticky mud and sink holes. Here you can also visit the **Bermuda Glass Blowing Studio**, 16 Blue Hole Hill. It is open daily from 9am to 5pm between April and December and 10am to 4pm Tuesday to Saturday from January to March. Glass blowing takes place between 9am and noon and 1pm to 4pm. There are glass workshops on Sunday ☎ 293-2234.

Then take the causeway across Castle Harbour, past airport to **Ferry Reach** and the **Bermuda Biological Station for Research**. This is a world-famous research center which has been studying global environmental changes, the Gulf Stream, marine biology, oceanography and mariculture for almost a century. There are free guided tours at 10am every Wednesday ☎ 297-1880.

The road then crosses the swing bridge and runs around **Mullet Bay** into **St George's Town**.

St George's Town

St George's was Bermuda's first settlement and capital, and is a genuinely, charming compact town full of wonderful old buildings, twisting alleys and historical intrigue. It is easy and fun to explore on foot. The settlement dates from 1609 making it the second oldest English settlement in the New World after Jamestown in Virginia. For more than 200 years it was the heart of the island with the main Harbour and all the Government offices including customs and tax collection, and this was partly responsible for its downfall. All ships were required to report to the customs house to pay any taxes due on their cargo, but many captains and ship owners had homes around the Great Sound and preferred to anchor there and, at the same time, avoiding the revenue men in St George's. To counter this lost revenue the authorities ordered that a harbor be built at Hamilton to supervise vessels in the Great Sound. This quay rapidly grew and the settlement expanded until it became so commercially and politically important that the capital was transferred from St George's.

Above: St Peter's Church, St George's
Below: King's Square, St George's

A walking tour of the town of St George's

The original town was even smaller than present day St George's because much of the waterfront and all of **King's Square** was marshland until the last century when it was reclaimed. Today King's Square is the heart of the town and the place to start your walking tour.

Call in first at the tourist office where there are excellent leaflets and maps of the town as well as all the information about current events and activities.

There are a number of other points of interest around the square including the two-floor **Town Hall**, built in 1808 and faithfully restored to its former glory with local cedar wood panels. It now houses the town's administration and there are pictures and paintings of many former mayors. It is open daily from Monday to Saturday between 10am and 4pm, and admission is free ☎ 297-1532.

The second floor **Town Hall Theatre** presents *Bermuda Journey*, a multi-screen slide presentation of Bermuda's history. It is open from Monday

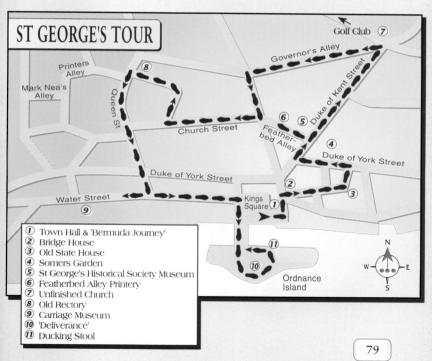

ST GEORGE'S TOUR

Golf Club ⑦
Governor's Alley
Printers Alley
Mark Nea's Alley
Queen St
⑧
Duke of Kent Street
Church Street
Feather-bed Alley
⑥ ⑤
④
Duke of York Street
Duke of York Street
② ③
Water Street
Kings Square ①
⑨
⑪
⑩
Ordnance Island

N
W — E
S

① Town Hall & 'Bermuda Journey'
② Bridge House
③ Old State House
④ Somers Garden
⑤ St George's Historical Society Museum
⑥ Featherbed Alley Printery
⑦ Unfinished Church
⑧ Old Rectory
⑨ Carriage Museum
⑩ 'Deliverance'
⑪ Ducking Stool

to Saturday between 11.15am and 3.15pm but hours may be limited between December and April so check first. There is an admission charge ☎ 297-1642.

Also worth visiting is the **Carole Holding Studio Print and Craft Shop**, which displays and sells the work of local artists and craftsmen. It is open from 9am to 5pm Monday to Saturday and from 11am to 5pm on Sunday. Admission is free ☎ 297-1833.

The early 18th century **Bridge House**, 1 Bridge Street, just off King's Square, is a Bermuda National Trust property, and now home to a privately run art gallery and craft shop. It gets its name because there used to be a bridge over a small creek which was drained as part of the reclamation work last century. For many years the property was one of the official residences of the island's Governors. The house is open from Monday to Saturday between 10am and 5pm, and during the summer only from 11am to 3pm on Sunday. Admission is free ☎ 297-8211.

King Street runs east from the square and you can visit **Buckingham**, an early Georgian building dating from the mid-18th century. Now run by the Bermuda National Trust, it is leased to a candle and gift shop.

Next door is **Reeve Court**, another fine Bermuda National Trust property. Although the house is not open to the public you can visit the garden.

The Old State House

At the end is Princess Street and the **Old State House**, the oldest stone building in Bermuda. It was built in the 1620s by Governor Nathaniel Butler from local limestone, and the builders used lime mixed with turtle oil for mortar. As soon as it was finished it became the home of the island's parliament which until then, had been meeting in St Peter's Church. After Hamilton became the capital and a new Sessions House was built, the Old State House was rented to the Masons for a token 'peppercorn' rent. It is now the Masonic Lodge of St George No. 200 of the Grand Lodge of Scotland. It is open on Wednesday from 10am to 4pm and the day of the Annual Ceremonial Handing over of the Peppercorn Rent in April. There is no telephone.

Somers Garden

Continue inland along Princess Street to **Somers Garden** so named because the heart of Sir George Somers is said to be buried there. After being shipwrecked on Bermuda in 1609 he oversaw the building of the *Deliverance*, a replica of which can be seen on Ordnance Island, and sailed on to his original destination of Jamestown in Virginia. When he arrived there he found the colony was short of supplies so he returned to Bermuda where unfortunately, he was taken ill and died.

According to legend nephew Matthew was asked to bury the heart in Bermuda but whether his uncle's wishes were carried out remains a mystery. It is known that Matthew smuggled his uncle's body aboard a ship because seamen considered it bad luck to have a dead person on board, and that Sir George was buried near the family home in Dorset, England. Whatever the truth, Sir George's spirit lives on in Bermuda.

Turn left into Duke of York Street for **Fort William** which was built in the early 19th century as the town's new powder store following the successful raid on the old arsenal by pro-American supporters. The massive walls and huge doors were intended to prevent any further raids.

Then right into Duke of Kent Street for **Featherbed Alley** and the **St George's Historical Society Museum** in a typical 18th century Bermudian structure. It contains period furnishings and many historic articles and documents. One of the most curious exhibits is a raft designed to carry torpedoes during the American Civil war.

The raft was being towed by a Union ship and was to have been used to blow up the defensive boom across Charleston Harbor. During a storm the raft broke free and was eventually beached in Bermuda, and it was many more years before the mystery surrounding the raft was solved. The delightful cottage gardens behind the museum are worth a visit. Both are open Monday to Friday from 10am to 4pm and there is a small admission charge for the museum ☎ 297-0423.

Also in the alley is the **Featherbed Alley Printery** with its ancient printing press. It is open from 10am to 4pm Monday to Saturday and admission is free

☎ 297-0878. Also of interest is **St George's Art and Craft Shop** in Featherbed Alley, which displays the arts and crafts of local artists and artisans. It is open from 10am to 4pm Monday to Saturday ☎ 297-0033.

Continue along Duke of Kent Street beyond its junctions with Church Folly Lane to The **Unfinished Church** at the top of Duke of Kent Road. Work was started in 1870 as a replacement for St Peter's, but the magnificent Gothic folly was never finished and the remaining funds were used to help pay for the new Trinity Church in Hamilton. The building was acquired by the Bermuda National Trust in 1992 and work is underway to restore and stabilize the structure. Do not enter the church but appreciate it from the safety of the path.

Return downtown by taking Governor's Alley and then turning left into Clarence Street down to its junction with Church Street. About half way along Church Street is Broad Alley and the **Old Rectory**, another Bermuda National Trust property. Built at the end of the 17th century by George Dew – said to have been a reformed pirate – it was for more than 50 years until 1805, the home of Alexander Richardson, vicar of St Peter's. It is now a private home but the house and garden are open on Wednesday from noon to 5pm and admission is free, although donations are welcomed ☎ 297-0878.

Broad Alley runs to Queen

Unfinished Church, St George's

St Peter's Church

Return to Church Street for the 18th century **St Peter's Church** and churchyard which stand on the oldest church site in the Western Hemisphere. The cedar fitted church, parts of which date back to 1620, was influenced by the architectural style of Sir Christopher Wren who built London's St Paul's Cathedral, and has a wonderful facade. It stands on the site of a wooden church built in 1612 but destroyed by a hurricane.

The church was enlarged in 1713 and again in 1833 when the two lateral galleries were added, and the cedar altar is the oldest piece of carving on the island. The church contains many treasures including a 500 year old baptismal font, a Charles I chalice (a gift from the Bermuda Company) and a William of Orange communion set. The churchyard has many fascinating tombstones and offers a mini history of St George's with the graves of governors and lovers, and gun runners and slaves.

Hester 'Nea' Tucker is buried in the Tucker family vault, and there is an elaborate memorial to 20 years old US Navy Midshipman Dale killed in a battle with the British Royal Navy in 1812. The gnarled cedar tree is said to have been growing on the site since at least 1620 and the original church bell hung from one of its boughs. A piece of wood from the tree was used to fashion the gavel used by the Speaker in the Sessions House. The church is open daily from 9.30am to 5pm and admission is free ☎ 297-8359.

Street with Printer's Alley opposite. It was here that the island's first newspaper, the Bermuda Gazette was printed in 1784. Running off Printer's Alley is **Nea's Alley**, the subject of another charming island romance. The alley used to be called Cumberland Lane and poet Thomas Moore, who was born in Dublin in 1779 and was a close friend of Lord Byron, lived there for four months while employed as Registrar of the Admiralty Court. During this time he met and fell in love with Hester, the wife of William Tucker, who lived next door. Moore called her Nea and refers to her in many of his poems. In such a small community, such a liaison could not go unnoticed and Moore left the island and returned to work in London. Nea died in 1817 at the age of 31.

Exit in Duke of York Street. Almost opposite is the Bermuda National Trust **Confederate Museum** in the former Globe Hotel. This was built at the beginning of the 18th century with public funds raised by Governor Day who then tried to claim it as his home. It became a hotel in the mid-19th century. During the American Civil War Bermuda was very much on the side of the South and the hotel was used by Confederate Agents to charter ships to carry supplies to beat the blockade of the southern US ports. The museum has period furnishings, blockade running maps, memorabilia and interpretive displays. It is open from Monday to Saturday from 9.30am to 4.30pm April to October and from 10am to 4pm from November to March. There is a small admission charge ☎ 297-1423.

Opposite is the **Carriage Museum** containing the Wilkinson Collection. Before the railway opened in 1931, carriages were the principal means of getting around and carrying goods. As a result, there is a large and beautifully restored collection of horse drawn vehicles on display, from elegant Victorian carriages, surreys with fringes, to children's pony carts and four horse country brakes. The museum is open from Monday to Friday and some Saturdays between 10am

Tucker House

Head west along Duke of York Street past Barber's Alley to Water Street and the **Tucker House**, the home of Henry Tucker, President of the Governor's Council from 1775 to 1800. The house, built of limestone in 1711 and noted for its high ceilings and use of pine, is furnished with many heirlooms donated in 1950 by Robert Tucker of the Maryland Tuckers from Baltimore. It includes period silver, cedar and mahogany furniture, paintings and artifacts, and an archaeological exhibit discovered during excavations beneath the basement floor.

In a small room off the study, the free slave Joseph Hayne Rainey, set up a barber's shop before returning to the United States in 1866 where four year later, he became the first black elected member of the House of Representatives, (thus the name of Barber's Alley). The house is open from Monday to Saturday from 10am to 4pm from April to October and from 10am to 4pm November to March. There is a small admission charge ☎ 297-0545.

and 5pm and while admission is free, donations are welcomed ☎ 297-1367.

The Carriage Museum stands between Water Street and **Somer's Wharf** where the cruise ships dock and the attractive area has many shops and eateries, including the Carriage House Restaurant.

Then head back to King's Square along Water Street and cross the bridge to visit **Ordnance Island**. You can go aboard the *Deliverance*, a full size replica of the 17th century ship that carried the 1609 survivors of the wrecked *Sea Venture* on to their original destination of Jamestown in Virginia. The original vessel was built at nearby Buildings Bay and was fashioned from salvaged pieces of the *Sea Venture* and island cedar – a remarkable feat. You can tour the *Deliverance* daily for a small admission charge. It is open from Monday to Saturday between 9am and 6pm (10am and 4pm Nov to March) ☎ 297-1459.

Close to the *Deliverance* is the replica ducking stool which looks out over Convict Bay, and on the western tip of the small island is a statue of Sir George Somers, the settlement's founder.

As you cross back into King's Square, you can drop in at the waterside **White Horse Tavern**. Now a popular restaurant, it was the home of prominent merchant John Davenport, the subject of much local folklore. It is said that shortly after arriving in St George's around 1815, he opened a provisions store on the square and won the lucrative contract to supply the garrison. He kept his money in a wooden barrel under his bed and when one barrel was full he removed it to the cellar and replaced it with an empty one. After he died, a fortune in gold and silver was discovered hidden in his cellar.

Leaving town

On the north coast of St George's is **Tobacco Bay** where in 1775 gunpowder stolen from the St George's Armoury was rowed out to ships bound for Boston during the American Revolution. Bermuda was sympathetic to the American cause and many powerful Bermudian families such as the Tuckers, had relatives living in the American colonies. Bermuda's problem was that Congress had banned all trade with British colonies and the island needed to import grain from America. A delegation was sent to Philadelphia offering salt in exchange for beef. The Americans made it quite clear that saltpeter would be more welcome than salt, so the Bermundians returned with some of their American relatives, raided the armory and stole 100

• Fort St Catherine •

On the north eastern corner of the island the beaches of **Achilles Bay** and **St Catherine Beach** surround the massive stone **Fort St Catherine**. Work on the fort began in 1614 on the orders of Governor Richard Moore, and continued for almost 300 years on the headland with sappers excavating many tunnels in the rock. The present structure was built between 1820 and 1870 with drawbridge and moat, ramparts and formidable firepower. It now contains a military museum with historical dioramas, weapons collection, replicas of the Crown Jewels and the only known 40lb (18kg) guns still on their original carriages. It is also the home of George, the ghost. The views from the ramparts are breathtaking. There is a short audio visual presentation about the fort which is open daily from 10am to 4pm. There is an admission charge ☎ 297-1920.

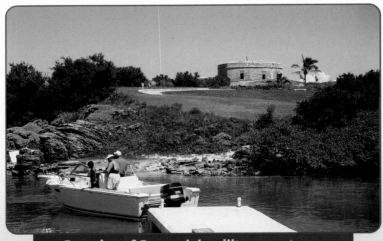

Remains of Bermuda's military past can be seen throughout the island

barrels of gunpowder which were smuggled to the Americans past the British Royal Navy blockade. Shortly afterwards, normal trade between America and Bermuda was resumed. Today the sheltered bay offers great snorkeling and you can wade out to the coral formations. There is a cafe and

Above: The white sands and shallow seas are ideal for families with young children

changing rooms, and snorkeling gear can be rented. It is a popular beach for families because of the safe waters.

Barry Road runs down the eastern side of St George's Island past **Fort Albert**. This was built to protect Bermuda from George Washington's troops. It leads to **Buildings Bay,** so named because the *Deliverance* was built there, and **Gates Fort**, a reconstruction of the sort of small fortification that surrounded St George's in the first half of the 17th century. It was originally called Davers Fort but renamed after

Thomas Gates who was the first of the *Sea Ventures* crew to struggle ashore. The fort is open daily and admission is free. A little further along the coast road is the rather ugly Alexandra Battery, built in the mid-19th century with formidable fortifications, some of which remain.

You can return on **Cut Road** which follows the western coast of the peninsula back into St George's, and then on over the swing bridge back on to **St David's Island.**

The huge US Naval Air Station which started operations in

the Second World War closed in 1995. You can visit the stone and cedar **Carter House** built about 1640 by the descendants of Christopher Carter, one of the three survivors of the *Sea Venture* who volunteered to remain on Bermuda when the *Deliverance* sailed. There is a legend that the three men found a huge quantity of valuable ambergris washed up on the beach and hid it in the hope of smuggling it back to England where it could be sold for a fortune. Carter spilled the beans to Governor Moore and as a reward was granted Cooper's Island. Originally a separate island, Cooper Island became a part of St David's because of land reclamation while the US base was being built. The house with period furnishings, is normally open on Wednesday between 11am and 3pm, but it

is advisable to ring first to check and get details on regulations for entry to the base ☎ 297-1150.

Clearwater Beach and neighboring **Turtle Beach** stand at the end of the airport's runway and are clearly signposted through the former US Naval Air Station. Both beaches offer safe swimming with lifeguards on duty during the summer, plus changing rooms, toilets, picnic areas, concession stands and a hiking trail along the coast.

St David's Head stands at the southern end of St David's Island and is capped by the lighthouse which stands on **Lighthouse Hill.** The recently refurbished **St David's Lighthouse** is made of Bermuda stone and dates from 1879, and is usually open from Monday to Saturday from May to September. Admission is free

Crystal Caves

The **Crystal Caves** are off the main road on Wilkinson Avenue, and in the grounds of the Grotto Bay Beach Hotel and Tennis Club. The complex of caves and underground lakes was discovered in 1907 by two boys looking for a lost ball. The cavernous caves are filled with weird limestone formations including stalactites and stalagmites, and how they are formed is explained as part of the guided tour. The caves get their name because the water in the lakes, although 55 feet (17m) deep, is crystal clear. They are open daily from 9.30am to 4.30pm. There is an admission charge ☎ 293-0640.

☎ 236-4201. On the end of the peninsula is **St David's Battery** which was formidable in its day, able to propel shells from its 9 inch (23 cm) guns more than 20 miles (32km) out to sea. Today it is more famous as the finishing line for the prestigious Bermuda yacht race.

You have to retrace your journey back across the island, across the Causeway and then turn left on Harrington Sound Road.

Tom Moore's Tavern on Walsingham Lane, is named after the Irish poet of Nea's Alley fame mentioned in the walking tour of St George's. The original house was called Walsingham after one of the *Sea Venture's* survivors, and was expanded in the 17th century by Samuel Trott. A later relative also called Samuel Trott befriended Moore who became a frequent visitor to the house which is set in wooded grounds. Moore used to sit under a calabash tree composing his poems. It was also under this tree that a group of islanders decided to establish the Royal Bermuda Yacht Club. Behind the tavern is Tom Moore's Jungle, a lovely wooded area with some spectacular views.

The road then passes **Walsingham Bay** and arrives at **Leamington Caves**.

The road south then passes **Shark Hole** and the **Castle Harbour Golf Club** to reach

Leamington Caves

Leamington Caves on the Harrington Sound Road. While not as impressive as Crystal Caves they are still worth a visit for their unusual limestone formations. They are open from Monday to Saturday between 9.30am and 4pm. There is an admission charge ☎ 293-1188. If you have lunch at the excellent nearby Plantation Restaurant (and spend more than $10) you get free admission to the caves.

Tucker's Town. It is named after Governor Daniel Tucker who tired of St George's in 1616 and wanted to move the capital to what is now Tucker's Town. Work started with some streets laid and a few houses built by the water, but the idea had little support and Tucker's Town was little more than a small fishing village until the 1920s when the Furness and Withy Shipping Line bought some land and built the luxurious Mid Ocean Club. This was followed by the Castle Harbour Resort now owned by Marriott. Club members then started to build their own luxury vacation homes. Tucker's Town is now the most expensive and exclusive part of the island.

Tucker's Town Bay lies to the north of the peninsula which stretches out across the mouth of Castle Harbour with the **Castle Islands Nature Reserve** at its tip. **King's Castle** is one of these islands and was fortified by Governor Moore in 1612-13 to protect the entrance to the Harbour. The fort saw action the following year when it fired two cannonballs at two approaching Spanish galleons. Neither hit but the Spanish vessels sailed away which was just as well for it is claimed that the fort had only one more cannonball left in its arsenal.

Along the South Shore Road there is a sign directing you to the **Natural Arches,** two weather and sea eroded limestone arches which stand by the beach.

Take South Road west past **Trott's Pond** and **Mangrove Lake** where you have a choice. You can then either take Harrington Sound Road back to Hamilton or your resort, or follow tour 1, picking it up at the Devil's Hole Aquarium.

St David's Lighthouse

This tour can be completed in a number of ways depending on your starting point. It takes in the parishes of **Paget, Warwick, Southampton** and **Sandys,** many of the fine beaches along the south shore, the more rural west end and the settlement of Somerset Village and the historic Naval Dockyard. If you are staying in or around the capital, you can take the ferry across to the Dockyard and island hop back. Better still, explore the western half of the island by scooter or bicycle travelling through Paget, Warwick and Southampton parishes and then visiting Sandys and Somerset Village before touring the Dockyard and returning from there by ferry to Hamilton.

You need a full day to take in this tour and spread it over two days if you want to stop off for cooling swims and leisurely lunches.

Waterville

If proceeding by road from Hamilton you follow the shoreline round to **Waterville** which stands at the foot of Hamilton Harbour and is a splendid 18th century Georgian home with period furnishing and chandeliered dining room, set in lush grounds with lawns, rose garden, shady tamarinds and palms. It is now the headquarters of the Bermuda National Trust Properties and is steeped in history. In 1842 it was the first store opened by the Trimingham family, and it later became an inn in which essayist E.B. White and writer James Thurber stayed. It is one of seven historic properties run by the Bermuda National Trust. The house is open from 9am to 5pm Monday to Friday and the gift shop from 10am to 4pm Tuesday to Friday ☎ 236-6483.

The Botanical Gardens

The **Botanical Gardens** are in Point Finger Road. From Middle Road, take Tee Street, then Berry Hill Road and after about one mile (1.6km) turn left into Point Finger Road. Call in at the Visitor Centre first. The gardens, which covered 10 acres (4 hectares) when they opened in 1898, now boast more than 1,000 species of plants and trees in its 36 lush acres (14 hectares). Apart from indigenous species, almost all the plants were brought to the island by seafarers during the 18th and 19th centuries. There are several permanent collections including the exotic orchid house, hibiscus display, sub tropical fruit groves, formal garden and the native cedar and Banyan trees. There is an aviary and an aromatic Garden for the Blind, as well as a gift shop and cafe. The gardens are open year round from sunrise to sunset and there are guided tours at 10.30am on Tuesday, Wednesday and Friday from April to October and Tuesday and Friday from November to March. Admission is free (except for the three days of the annual agricultural show) but donations are welcomed ☎ 236-4201.

The Gardens are also the location of **Camden**, the elegant official residence of the Prime Minister. The white building dates from around 1775 but was greatly embellished during the Victorian era. Henry Tucker, Mayor of Hamilton, bought the property in 1823 and built in arrowroot factory behind the house. The verandah, porch and bay windows were added by his son Thomas. The house contains many fine antiques and early Bermuda furnishings and furniture. The portraits of four Bermuda Prime Ministers hang at the top of the impressive cedar staircase. The house is open on Tuesday and Friday between noon and 2.30pm, provided there are no official functions, and admission is free ☎ 236-5732.

Close to the **Lower Ferry Landing** on Harbour Road is **Clermont**, a fine house which

also lays claim to having the island's first tennis court in 1871. It was the home of Sir Brownlow Gray, the island's Chief Justice. The house is not open to the public but it is worth viewing from the outside.

Further west in Great Sound you can make out Darrell's Island where hundreds of South Africans died while prisoners during the Boer War.

Three roads run through Paget and Warwick Parishes – Harbour Road which follows the southern shores of Great Sound past the Belmont and Riddells Bay Golf Clubs; Middle Road which runs down the middle of the island; and South Shore Road which follows the south coast and is the most scenic of the three very pretty routes. There are many side roads connecting all three, so you can criss cross from one shore to the other very easily.

One of these is Valley Road which runs between Harbour Road and Middle Road and can be taken to visit **St Paul's Church**. The present structure dates from 1796 and replaced an earlier church on the site. The church is open Monday to Friday from 8am to 4.30pm and admission is free ☎ 236-5880. The church overlook **Paget Marsh**, an area of woodlands, marsh and mangrove, that must look today very much as it did when the first settlers arrived almost 500 years ago. It is administered by the Bermuda National Trust and can be visited by arrangement ☎ 236-6483. Recently, 26 acres (10.5 hectares) of the marsh was opened as a nature reserve with boardwalk access.

From the Botanic Gardens, the South Shore Road passes **Hungry Bay** with its nature reserve and mangrove swamps (best visited with a guide), and **Grape Bay**, with side roads off to **Elbow Beach** famous for its coral pink sands. The western half of the beach is public and Dinty's lunch wagon provides refreshments, or you can use the facilities of the Elbow Beach Hotel for a small charge.

If you cut inland to Middle Road on Tribal Road 2 and Ord Road you can visit **Christ Church** which dates from 1719, and is believed to be the oldest Presbyterian church in any British colony.

The South Shore Road continues past **Warwick Camp** built in the 1870s and used as a rifle range and training area during the First World War, the **Southampton Princess Hotel** and its **Princess Golf Club**. One of the island's latest attractions

Beaches and Coves

The South road runs quite close to the coast past a string of fabulous beached including **Coral Beach** and **Marley Beach**. **Astwood Park Beach and Park** has open picnic areas with tables among the trees and a sandy cove for swimming. The cliffs behind are home to the elegant longtails.

Warwick Long Bay has a long white stretch of sand with toilets and a lunch wagon nearby on South Shore Road.

Jobson Cove, Stonehole Bay and **Chaplin Bay** are sheltered secluded coves with huge boulders towering out of the sea.

South Shore Road then passes **Peel Bay** and **Horseshoe Bay**, the island's best known and most popular beach with cafes, toilets, changing rooms, watersports and lifeguards. The land between the road and the coast makes up the **South Shore Park.**

There are so many excellent beaches along this stretch of coast that if you get to one that is too busy for your liking, you can always continue on for a little way and be likely to find your own secluded cove.

is **Dolphin Quest**, owned by the hotel. It is a 3 acre (1 hectare) natural habitat dolphinarium and education facility in a natural sea inlet. It currently has seven Atlantic bottle nose dolphins. Visitors can pay to get a behind-the-scenes tour and put their names forward for the chance to swim with the dolphins.

The **Gibbs Hill Lighthouse** – also known as the Parish Lantern – stands on Gibbs Hill, off Lighthouse Road. It was the second cast-iron lighthouse ever constructed and the oldest in existence, and has been warning ships since 1846 from its vantage point 362 feet (110m) above sea level. You can climb the tower to the observation platform if you have the puff and a head for heights. It is open daily from 9am to 4.30pm and there is an admission charge ☎ 238-0524.

The South Shore Road continues past more lovely beaches at **Sinky Bay**, **Boat Bay**, **Christian Bay** and **Church Bay**, which is small but lovely and good for snorkeling. It then turns inland to connect with Middle Road which is the main route through the West End running all the way to Somerset Bridge and Somerset Landing where you catch the Hamilton ferry. It is worth visiting the Bermuda Triangle Brewery, a micro brewery on Industrial Park Road off Middle Road. It

is open for tours and tastings weekdays at 4pm and on Saturdays at noon and 3pm.

As you continue west after joining Middle Road you have Little Sound on your right and Five Star Island just offshore. You then pass Frank's Bay, Jennings Bay and Evans Bay all in Little Sound and across the water you can see the US Naval Air Station Annex on a peninsula which juts out into Great Sound.

There are side roads on your left down to tiny **West Whale Bay**, with its pink beach, Whitney Bay, and past the Port Royal Golf Course there is a road down to Pompano Beach Club's Watersports Centre. It is worth taking the road down the hill to **Whale Bay Fort**, a small fort built in the 19th century, which overlooks a lovely secluded beach which can only be reached on foot. The fort was built to defend Hog Fish Cut, one of the few safe channels for shipping through the reefs. The bay gets its name because it was the middle of the island's whaling industry.

Middle Road continues past Wreck Road on the left which goes to Wreck Hill and then reaches **Somerset Bridge**, the world's smallest drawbridge. The actual section of bridge that raises is only 22 inches (56cm) wide, just enough to let a ship's mast through. The

**Above: Gibbs Hill lighthouse
Below: Early Bermuda
Weather Stone**

which caused a storm of protest. He was summoned back to London to explain his actions. In the compromise settlement, the Governor was allowed to keep the plot on which his house stood and the rest of the land was donated to the church. The house has long since disappeared.

The bridge takes you on to Somerset Island in Sandy's Parish. Sandy was one of the original Bermuda Company investors, and Somerset is not named after the English county, but after Sir George Somers. It used to be known as Somers Estate, and this was abridged over the years to Somerset.

Sheltered **Ely's Harbour** is on your left and has pleasure boat, marina, snorkeling and water-ski facilities.

original bridge dates from the 17th century.

Just before the bridge you pass a side road called **Overplus**, which leads to a small plot of prime land which featured prominently in Bermudian history. When the island was divided up into 'tribes' by Richard Norwood for the Bermuda Company, there was a parcel of 200 acres (81 hectares) which was surplus. Governor Tucker asked Norwood to look out for a suitable plot of land which he could acquire to use this surplus up. Norwood selected this site and Tuckerhad a house built on it

Scar Hill Fort

Proceeding towards Somerset Village, on your right you can see **Scaur Hill Fort** set on one of the highest points on Somerset Island. It offers commanding views across the Great Sound. Work started on the fort in 1868 and took 10 years to complete. It was one of a series of forts built along a huge defensive ditch designed to protect the Royal Naval Dockyard from forces attacking overland.

The fort with its old moat and massive stone walls is set in 22 acres (9 hectares) of parkland with picnic areas and trails. British soldiers were garrisoned there until the end of the First World War, and during the Second World War a US army coastal artillery battery was stationed at the fort. Little remains of the fort, but the grounds are open and views are there to be enjoyed. It is open daily from 10am to 4.30pm and admission is free ☎ 234-0908.

The Heydon Trust is another nature reserve off Somerset Road, opposite Willowbank. There are more than 40 acres (16 hectares) of gardens, flower and vegetable areas and citrus groves all protected as a bird sanctuary. There are paths through the reserve and one leads to the delightful, small Heydon Chapel, said to date from the early 17th century, and still used for services. The reserve is open from dawn to dusk Monday to Saturday ☎ 234-1831.

St James Church

The church, with its elegant steeple, stands atop the hill and the entrance off the main road is marked by a pair of gates said to have been designed by a Royal Engineer officer stationed at the dockyard in 1872. The church dates from 1789 and replaced a wooden building destroyed by a hurricane in 1780. The steeple is a replica of the original 1880 structure which came crashing down in 1937 after being struck by lightning. The steeple was designed by Dr Henry Hinson, an island physician and talented amateur architect. He also designed the spires for St Mark's, St Paul's in Paget and St Paul's in Hamilton.

Somerset Road then leads to the **Somerset Island Visitor Centre**, open from 9am to 3pm

April to mid-November, and after a few minutes you reach the impressive arched gateway into the **Springfield Plantation House.** Adjacent is the **Gilbert Nature Reserve** – this 5-acre (2-hectare) reserve is heavily wooded and formerly part of the Springfield Plantation founded around 1700. Both are now owned by the Bermuda National Trust and the house and outbuildings are being restored. The property was owned by the Springfield family from the beginning of the 18th century until they sold it in 1973. The reserve is always open and admission is free ☎ 236-6483.

Somerset Village

This is the main settlement on the western side of the island. While certainly not large, it has a post office, police station, two banks, some shops and a handful of restaurants for the tourists passing through on their way to and from the Dockyard. The village also serves a large numbers of Bermudians who have chosen to live on Somerset Island rather than in more built up areas, and many of the side roads off the main Somerset Road lead to small residential communities. Freight used to be shipped in to the public wharf. The old cedar hoist, dating from the early 19th century, which unloaded it, still stands.

You can take the ferry from Hamilton to Watford Bridge to join the Walking Tour of Somerset which takes place every Thursday at 10am from November to March. It leaves from the **Country Squire** and take in many of the area's historic homes. A fascinating aspect of the walk is that you are told about local history, architecture and the former curative uses of many of the plants, herbs and flowers you can see along the way.

There are lots of secluded coves and fine beaches around the island, especially **Somerset** and **Long Bay** on the north coast east of **Daniel's Head.** North west of Somerset Village

Long Bay's Bird Reserve

The area around Long Bay is a public park and nature reserve, with a bird reserve alongside owned by the Bermuda Audubon Society. This peninsula is an important landing point for birds on spring and autumn migration and many rare species are regularly seen. You can also spot warblers, herons, egrets, kingfishers, ducks and purple gallinule, plus cardinals, chick of the village and catbirds.

on Cambridge Road is **Cambridge Beaches**, the island's original cottage colony.

For those not interested in the wildlife, Long Bay has a great beach where you can swim or enjoy a picnic. The park is always open.

Daniel's Head Road runs past **Skeeter's Corner** named after Edward Skeeter who lived with his wife in a cottage nearby. In 1878 he murdered her and threw the body off the headland into the water. He then confessed to police and said the only reason he had done it was because she talked too much.

Offshore is **Daniel's Island** and more of the **Sea Gardens** which surround the north western and northern coast of Bermuda.

Watford Bridge takes you to **Watford Island** and nearby **Boaz Island**. Both islands are quite small and while they do not have much to offer the visitor unless you are interested in bird watching, there are good views over sweeping **Mangrove Bay**.

Grey's Bridge leads you on to **Ireland Island** which is really two islands. Ireland Island South is separated from Ireland Island North by The Cut Bridge and you cross this to get to the Dockyard. Most of Ireland Island South is fringed by mangroves and lagoons which make up **Lagoon Park**, and there are

paths for those interested in birdwatching.

Some way past the 19th century **Royal Navy Cemetery** on your left is a bridge over a cut which runs from the lagoon to the ocean. In the early 19th century, a naval surgeon noticed there were many cases of yellow fever and he thought the stagnant waters of the nearby lagoon was to blame. By having the cut built, tidal waters were able to flush out the lagoon, and at the same time they swept out to sea the mosquito larvae which were responsible for the disease.

The Royal Naval Dockyard

The **Royal Naval Dockyard** was started in 1809 and the Duke of Wellington was determined to make it the 'Gibraltar of the West' to defend Britain's interests against any threats from Napoleon. The fortified dockyard covered 75 acres (30 hectares) and contains many spectacular buildings built with the sweat and blood of slaves and English convicts who were often worked to death. The convicts' cemetery is on Cochrane Road. The fort opened in 1814 and one of its first acts was to launch a naval raid on the American capital of Washington. For almost 200 years it functioned as a naval dockyard and base until it was closed in 1951.

Historic Royal Naval Dockyard

Over the last few years it has been meticulously restored, and today it is a magnificent complex with the **Clocktower** shopping mall, restaurants, pub, marina and cruise ship terminal. The building with its three feet (1m) thick walls and twin 100 feet (30m) towers was finished in 1856 and originally were naval offices. The clock on the south tower was cast in England in 1857 by John Moore and Sons while the clock on the north tower was hand set daily to show the time of high tide, when it was safest for ships to enter and leave port. There is a **Visitor's Centre**, crafts market and **Art Centre, Bermuda Maritime Museum** and the historic **Commissioner's House** and entertainments for children and others who may not fully appreciate the Dockyard's living history. There are guided tours of the dockyard on Sunday afternoons between November and March.

The Queen's Exhibition Hall

Originally this was the dockyard's 19th century powder magazine and used to contain 5,000 barrels of gunpowder which is why it is surrounded by a moat which was an effective fire safety precaution and a deterrent to attackers. Today , it contains the **Bermuda Maritime Museum and Art Gallery** which stages exhibitions throughout the year. It was opened by Queen Elizabeth II in 1975.

The vast Bermuda Maritime Museum, entered over a dry moat and through the huge keep, covers 6 acres (2.4 hectares) of old powder houses, and features the story of the *Sea Venture* and other shipwrecks, boat building, whaling, pirate and privateers, and rum running, all part of the island's long and interesting maritime history.

Exhibits include articles salvaged from the wrecks of 16th century Spanish treasure ships, and relics from *Sea Venture*, whose ill fated voyage in 1609 led to the Bermuda's colonization by the English. Its two newest exhibits are the 'Age of Discovery' commemorating the 500th anniversary of Columbus's discovery of the New World, and the Bermuda Monetary Authority's display of the island's coinage from 1612. It is open daily from 10am (summer 9.30am) to 5pm and there is an admission charge ☎ 234-1418.

The **Commissioner's House** was built on the cliff in the 1820s and is the dockyard's oldest stone building, and is believed to be the world's oldest cast iron framed residence. It was the home of the Dockyard Commissioners until the late 1830s, and was then used as a barracks, and was actually commissioned by the *HMS Malabar* in 1919. It has been extensively restored.

The **Bermuda Art Centre** was opened by Princess Margaret in 1984 and has changing exhibitions featuring local artists. On display are paintings, photographs, island designed and hand dyed cloths, jewelry and sculptures. It is open from Tuesday to Saturday between 10am and 4pm, and on Sunday from noon to 5pm ☎ 234-2809.

The Dockyard's **Cooperage** built in 1830, now houses the cinema, Frog and Onion Pub and the **Bermuda Craft Centre** where you can see the island's talented artisans at work and buy their offerings. It is open daily from 10am to 5pm ☎ 234-3208. The Cooperage was built in 1831 and was vital as the only means of preserving supplies at sea was by salting them and storing them in barrels which needed to be repaired and replaced. There were two huge stone forges which were used to make the hoops for the barrels. The

Carole Holding Warehouse and Print Shop, Clocktower Building, also offers the chance to view and buy the work of local artists. It is open from 10am to 5pm Monday to Saturday and from 11am to 5pm on Sunday ☎ 234-3800.

Also of interest are the **Bermuda Children's Museum Society Room** near the Boat Loft entrance, where children can interact with the nautical exhibits; and the **Terrace Gallery** at 5 Dockyard Terrace, that features artists in residence.

The **Enterprise Submarine** also operates from the Dockyard offering close up underwater views of the reefs and shipwrecks. It operates from Sunday to Thursday between May and November and tenders (boats) ply between Hamilton and the Royal Naval Dockyard from 9am to 5pm. Reservations are required ☎ 234-3547.

On Sundays at 11.15am there are guided **nature walks** along 2 miles (3km) of scenic woodlands, seaside vistas, manicured parks and wildlife sanctuaries around the Dockyard.

3 EATING OUT

There is a remarkably large choice when it comes to eating out on the island. There are the inevitable fast food burger, pizza and fried chicken outlets, beach cafes offering excellent value for the money, and elegant upmarket dining rooms, as well as restaurants offering a wide range of ethnic cuisines, from traditional British to Caribbean and Indian to Chinese.

Note: Between November and March, many of Bermudas best restaurants offer a discount **Dine-Around** plan that allows visitors to sample the finest culinary offerings at a saving. Restaurants offer different meal plans, and all guests have to do is ring up the establishment, let them know you want the Dine-Around menu and book your table.

White Horse Tavern, St George's

Most accept credit cards and during peak times of the year, reservations for dinner are recommended. While prices vary enormously depending on the establishment, number of courses, wines chosen etc, expect to pay around $10 to $12 for a breakfast, $18 to $20 for a two course lunch, $30 for a three course dinner, $3 for a bottle of beer and the same for a glass of wine.

If you come across a restaurant not listed in the guide, or have comments about any of those that are, write to me c/o Gulf Atlantic Publishing, 1947 Lee Road, Winter Park, FL32789 USA.

The restaurants listed in the itineraries are classified by price – $ inexpensive, $$ moderate, $$$ expensive.

• Restaurants •

Ascot's $-$$

Royal Palms Hotel, corner of Rosemont Avenue and Richmond Road, Pembroke

☎ 295-9644

A lovely garden setting just outside Hamilton with a traditional English country pub-style bar and dining in or outside on the patio.

The Beergarden $$-$$$

Washington Lane, Hamilton

☎ 292-5516

Casual, fun dining with a mix of Caribbean food and German beer garden. It has great fish and seafood, red bean soup, low calorie, healthy dishes, and traditional Bermuda entrees like honey baked Chicken and home made chicken pie, and German specialties, such as bratwurst, goulash and Oktoberfest platter – a variety of German sausages with sauerkraut and mashed potatoes. It is open Monday to Saturday from 10am to 1am, and Sunday from 5pm.

Boat Bay Club $$-$$$

Sonesta Beach Hotel, Southampton

☎ 238-8122

Affectionately known as the BBC, the restaurant offers smart casual dining.

Cafe Lido $$

Elbow Beach Hotel

☎ 236-9884

An award-winning waterside terrace cafe with a Mediterranean cuisine, with dining in or out and an open air bar.

Caliban's $$-$$$

Ariel Sands Beach Club

☎ 236-1010

A great place to eat at any time of the day. Very good

wine list and live entertainment most nights.

Carriage House $$-$$$

Water Street, St George's

☎ 297-1730

Elegant dining in this historic brick vaulted restaurant, once the main island stores of the Royal Engineers, or outside on the wharfside terrace where you can watch the yachts and sip afternoon tea or enjoy an earlybird dinner or starlit feast.

Chancery Wine Bar $-$$

Chancery Lane, Hamilton

☎ 295-5058

A delightful cellar bar tucked away in Chancery Lane which runs between Front and Reid Streets with an imaginative lunch and dinner menu which changes monthly and an extensive list of wines.

Coconut Rock $-$$

Williams House,
Reid Street, Hamilton

☎ 292-1043

In the center of Hamilton and a popular meeting place where you can enjoy a varied menu or drink and take in the latest pop videos from the US and Europe.

Colony Pub $$-$$$

Princess Hotel

☎ 295-3000

Open daily for great value buffet lunch from noon to 2.30pm, and New York-style steak house with seafood for dinner.

Dennis's Hideaway $$$

Cashew City Road,
St David's

☎ 297-0044

Informal dining with the emphasis on informal but great Bermudian food with traditional dishes such as shark steaks.

Fisherman's Reef $$-$$$

Burnaby Street, just off Front Street, Hamilton

☎ 292-1609

Above the Hog Penny Pub and a popular eatery specializing in fresh fish, seafood and steaks.

Flanagan's $-$$

Emporium Building,
69 Front Street, Hamilton

☎ 295-8299

A traditional Irish Pub open daily.

Fourways Inn $$$

Highly recommended
1 Middle Road, Paget
☎ 236-6517

An award-winning island institution offering elegant, gracious dining from the extensive menu based on French and island cuisine. The 18th century Georgian property built of coral stone and cedar was for 200 years the home of the Harvey family. It has many fine period furnishings. There is dining inside or on the patio, and the restaurant is noted for its superb wine list and talented pianist. The food is superb. Jacket and tie is requested.

Fourways Pastry Shop $

Washington Mall,
Reid Street, Hamilton
☎ 295-3263

A great place for a quick fuel stop any time of the day with freshly prepared sandwiches and pizzas and freshly baked pastries.

Freddie's $-$$

King's Street, St George's
☎ 297-1717

An historic pub open all day for meals and Bermuda's largest selection of local and imported draft beers.

Freeport Seafood Restaurant $$

Royal Naval Dockyard
☎ 234-1692

Open daily from 9.30am to 11pm. Traditional pub food and try the Sunday morning codfish breakfast or the freshly squeezed mango juice.

Frog and Onion $-$$

Royal Naval Dockyard
☎ 234-2900

A traditional English-style pub with lovely large 18th century fireplace in what used to be the dockyard's cooperage.

Harbourfront $$-$$$

Front Street, Hamilton, opposite the ferry
☎ 295-4207

A lovely location with waterside views over Hamilton Harbour and specializing in fish, seafood and sushi.

Harley's $$-$$$

Princess Hotel
☎ 295-300

Named after Bermudian Harley Trott who in 1885 built and opened the island's first Princess Hotel which was named after HRH Princess Louise who had visited Bermuda in 1883.

The restaurant has a distinctly Mediterranean cuisine.

Henry VIII $$-$$$

South Shore Road, Southampton

☎ 238-1977

A popular and lively pub and restaurant overlooking the South Shore with Gibb's Hill Lighthouse above, to act as your beacon.

The Inlet $$-$$$

Palmetto Bay Hotel, Flatts Village

☎ 293-2323

This waterside restaurant is open all day from 8am to 9.30pm and its center of the island location makes it a great place to stop for lunch while out exploring. It offers full English breakfasts, pub fare, daily specials, low calorie, vegetarian dishes and a la carte dining with roast beef and Yorkshire pudding on Saturday and Sunday evenings. It is also a good place to enjoy a traditional Sunday codfish breakfast with all the trimmings.

Landfall $$-$$$

Clear View, Sandy Lane, Hamilton

☎ 293-1322

A delightful restaurant overlooking the sea in an old Bermuda home. You can dine in or out and enjoy island and international cuisine.

Lillian's $$-$$$

Soonest Beach Hotel, Southampton

☎ 238-8122

A very elegant restaurant with its art nouveau decor and specializing in the cuisine of Northern Italy.

Little Venice $$-$$$

Bermudian Road, Hamilton

☎ 295-3503

A very popular and good value Italian restaurant offering traditional meat and fish dishes.

Lobster Pot $$

6 Bermudiana Road, Hamilton

☎ 292-6898

An award winning Hamilton seafood restaurant which caters to its loyal local clientele as well as visitors.

Mikado $$-$$$

Castle Harbour Marriott, Paynter's Road, Tucker's Town

☎ 293-2040

The island's only Japanese

Above: Swizzle Inn
Below: King Square, St George's.
Freddies is on the left

restaurant with dishes prepared in front of you by the talented and skilled Teppanyaki and sushi chefs who have developed their cooking and knife wielding skills into a near cabaret act.

Monte Carlo $$-$$$

Victoria Street West, Hamilton

☎ 295-5453

A charming restaurant close to City Hall and specializing in southern European cuisine.

Newport Room $$$

Highly recommended

Southampton Princess Hotel

☎ 238-2555

Truly elegant dining in a gourmet restaurant noted for its French creations and stunning wine list. Starters include wonderful escargot, Scottish smoked salmon carved at the table, foie gras and marinated fillet of sturgeon. For main courses try roulade of roasted lobster and monkfish studded with asparagus and peppers served with garlic mashed potato in a vegetable trellis; fillet of salmon topped with a mushroom and herb duxelle broiled with fennel and set on raspberry butter; and double fillet of venison coated in a soft herb mousse

resting on a pumpkin and turnip puree, with wild cherry and juniper sauce. Finish off with a soufflé, crêpe suzette or one of the many other mouth watering dessert creations. The Newport Room is open for dinner from 6.30pm to 9.30pm (7pm to 10pm from June to September). Jacket and tie is required and reservations are recommended.

Newstead $$-$$$

Newstead Guest House

Harbour Road, Paget

☎ 236-6060

A lovely waterside restaurant with great food and stunning views.

Norwood Room $$-$$$

Stonington Beach Hotel

☎ 236-5416

Open for lunch and dinner prepared and served by the island's catering students under the attentive eyes of master chef tutors at the Hotel of the Hospitality and Culinary Institute of Bermuda.

Once Upon A Table $$$

Serpentine Road, Hamilton

☎ 295-8585

A charming restaurant in an old Bermuda home within

walking distance of the city center. Jacket and tie are required for dinner.

Ondine's $$$

Elbow Beach Hotel

South Shore Road, Paget

☎ 236-3535

Enjoy great buffet breakfasts from 7.30am and elegant casual dinners with seafood and steak specialties up to 9.30pm. Smart casual dining with jackets preferred and reservations recommended.

Paw Paws $$

87 South Shore Road, Warwick

☎ 236-7459

A bistro-type restaurant offering continental and Bermudian dishes.

Peg Leg Lounge $$

Fourways Inn

1 Middle Road, Paget

☎ 236-6517

This elegant restaurant is set in the large original kitchen with its stepped fireplace and offers tempting lunchtime dishes.

Pink's $

55 Front Street, Hamilton

☎ 295-3522

The place to have a sandwich, salad or hot dish and a

rest in between shopping and sightseeing in Hamilton.

Pirate's Landing $$-$$$

Royal Naval Dockyard

☎ 234-5151

International cuisine for lunch and dinner. Evening reservations are recommended. The walls are plastered with information and posters about infamous pirates, with pictures of a few locals thrown in to confuse!

Plantation $$-$$

Harrington Sound Road, Bailey's Bay

☎ 293-1188

A very traditional and popular Bermudian restaurant with log fires for cozy indoor dining on cooler evenings, or eating out under the stars in the lush gardens. Dress is smart casual.

Pompano Beach Club $-$$

Ocean front in Southampton, next to the Port Royal Golf Course

☎ 234-0222

A great place for an ocean front lunch and romantic dining with spectacular sunsets.

Port 'O' Call $$

87 Front Street, Hamilton

☎ 295-5373

Leisurely, informal dining on Hamilton's waterfront and open for lunch from Monday to Friday and dinner from Monday to Saturday.

Portofino $$

Bermudiana Road just off Front Street, Hamilton

☎ 292-2375

An Italian restaurant offering eat in and take away service.

Red Carpet $$-$$$

Armoury Building,
37 Reid Street, Hamilton

☎ (292-6195

A convenient and popular meeting place for a drink or Italian cuisine.

Ristorante Primavera $$

Pitt's Bay Road,
Hamilton West

☎ 295-2167

An elegant Italian restaurant noted for its pasta, seafood, oysters, wondrous sauces and mouthwatering desserts.

Robin Hood $

Richmond Road, Hamilton

☎ 295-3314

A great pub with atmosphere and good value food, darts, varied entertainment and sports bar.

Romancing The Scone $$

Above A.S. Cooper and Sons, Front Street, Hamilton

☎ 295-3961

Overlooking Front Street and Hamilton Harbour and offering snacks and hot dishes from breakfast to dinner.

The Seagrape $$-$$$

Sonesta Beach Hotel, Southampton

☎ 238-8122

Romantic terrace dining to the sound of Calypso music with great seafood, steaks and grilled dishes.

Southampton Princess

South Road, Southampton

☎ 238-2555

This large property offers six restaurants from the English-style Rib Room, seafood Whaler Inn, famous Waterlot Inn for gourmet dining, silver service Newport Room, casual Wicket's Brasserie, and dinner dancing at Windows on the Sound.

Spazzizi's $$-$$$

Elbow Beach Hotel
South Shore Road, Paget

☎ 236-3535

A bistro which offers breakfast, leisurely lunches and fun dining inside or on the terrace specializing in seafood.

Tio Pepe $$-$$$

Horseshoe Bay Beach, Southampton

☎ 238-1897

Very conveniently located at the entrance to the popular Horseshoe Beach and offering good value, tasty food from pasta and pizza to traditional Italian and island fare.

Tom Moore's Tavern

Walsingham Lane, Harrington Sound

☎ 293-8020

A lively restaurant steeped in history and with its own 'jungle' reserve out back.

Tree Frogs $$

Belmont Hotel, Middle Road, Warwick

☎ 236-1301

Good value dining all day from the buffet breakfast to dinner with a different menu every day.

Waterloo House $$-$$$

Pitt's Bay Road, Pembroke

☎ 295-4480

This former 19th century home is now a guest house and the all day, every day restaurant is noted for its hospitality, Bermudian and continental dishes.

Waterlot Inn $$-$$$

Middle Road, Southampton

☎ 238-2555

This historic 300 year old property features the very of Mediterranean and Bermudian cuisine. Jacket and tie are required for dinner.

White Horse Tavern $-$$

King's Square, St George's

☎ 297-1838

Overlooking the water and Ordnance Island, this pub restaurant makes a good place to catch your breath after exploring the town.

Windows On The Sound $$-$$$

Southampton Princess Hotel

☎ 238-2555

Elegant, sophisticated dining with a band for those who want to dance between courses, magnificent views to enjoy for those who don't.

Ye Olde Cock & Feather $$

Front Street, Hamilton

☎ 295-2263

A lively, busy pub and restaurant open daily from 11am to 1am.

ARRIVAL, ENTRY REQUIREMENTS AND CUSTOMS

Passports are the preferred document for entry although citizens of the United States and Canada can enter by producing proof of citizenship and identification, including photo ID.

For US visitors, the following items of identification are acceptable: US Passport containing a photograph that resembles the bearer, birth certificate with raised seal or certified copy, US re-entry permit, US voter's registration card, US Naturalization certificate or Green Card.

Canadian citizens may present either valid passport, birth certificate or certified copy, or Canadian Certificate of Citizenship.

Visitors from the UK and Western Europe must have a valid passport.

Visas are required from the nationals of most East European, African, Middle East and Asian countries, and visas and information about them can be obtained from the Visa Section of a British Passport Office or British Consulate.

All visitors must have a return or onward ticket, and entry may be denied without proof of onward travel.

An immigration card has to be filled in and presented on arrival. The form requires you to say where you will be staying on the island, and if you plan to move around, put down the first hotel you will be staying at. The immigration form is in two parts, one of which is stamped and returned to you in your passport. You must retain this until departure when the slip is retrieved as you check in at the airport.

If on business, a letter confirming this, may prove helpful in speeding your way through customs, especially if you are carring samples.

Having cleared immigration, you will have to go through customs, where you may have to make an oral declaration about whether you have goods to declare or not. You may be asked to open your luggage for inspection. If you have expensive cameras, or other personal items etc. it is a good idea to travel with a photocopy of the receipt.

Visitors entering Bermuda are allowed to bring in duty free: personal clothing, sports equipment, golf bags and cameras, plus 50 cigars, 200 cigarettes, 1lb (450 grams) of tobacco, 1 quart (1.137 liters) of liquor or wine.

Handy tip: Because of the price of beer and alcohol on the island, it is worth bringing in your full duty free allowance.

Do not bring in plants, fruits, vegetables or animals without an import permit from the Department of Agriculture, Fisheries and Parks. Their importation is strictly controlled in order to maintain the disease-free status of the islands.

Duty free

US Customs Pre-Clearance is available in Bermuda for all scheduled flights. All passengers departing to the US must fill out a written declaration before clearing US Customs in Bermuda. The forms are available from travel agencies and airline desks.

US citizens are allowed to take back up to US$400 worth of duty free goods if out of the country for more than 48 hours. The next US$1,000 is dutiable at 10 per cent, although gifts up to the value of US$50 can be mailed home duty-free. US visitors are also allowed as part of the duty-free allowance, five cartons of cigarettes and one liter of wine, liqueur or spirits.

Canadian citizens are allowed to take back $100 worth of duty free goods after 48 hours and any number of trips a year, or $300 worth after seven days away once every calendar year, as well as 200 cigarettes or equivalent, and 40 ounces of alcoholic drinks.

UK residents are allowed £136 or equivalent in duty free gifts, plus 200 cigarettes, 100 little cigars, 50 large cigars or 250 grams of tobacco and 1 liter of spirits and 2 liters of wine.

ACCOMMODATION

There is a wide range of accommodation to suit all tastes and pockets, from top class resort hotels to delightful guest houses, self-catering apartments. manor houses and cottages. The largest resort hotels have several hundred rooms and usually their own beach or beach club, while small hotels may have as few as 12 rooms and are highly individual. Cottage colonies are deluxe accommodations unique to Bermuda offering spectacular settings and amenities and featuring a main clubhouse with dining room, lounge and bar and cottages spread throughout the surrounding landscaped grounds offering privacy and luxury.

Housekeeping cottages and apartments are another option. The larger complexes are situated in landscape estates but without the central club house and have self catering facilities plus daily maid service. Some have a pool.

Most of the guest houses are old Bermuda homes in lush garden settings. A few have their own waterfront or pool and all offer friendly, informal living. A few guest houses have kitchenette units while others provide shared kitchen facilities for making snacks. Breakfast is usually the only meal provided.

Hotels offer a number of options for full meal plans to room only. If you want to eat out and explore quite a lot, it pays to stay in a hotel offering board only, or which includes the Dine-Around option, which allows you to eat out in several other establishments.

There are also apartments, holiday villas and beach cottages available for short and long rent offering you the privacy of your own accommodation and the flexibility to eat in or out, with cooks and maid service available if required.

Some terms: MAP stands for Modified American Plan i.e. breakfast and dinner are included. EP or European Plan means bed only and no meals and AP for American Plan, means room and all meals. Prices quoted by hotels are for rooms, whether one or two people are sharing, and you may find it difficult to get a reduction if you are alone, but have a go. $ represents inexpensive accommodation, $$ moderate, and $$$ de-luxe.

AN A-Z OF ACCOMMODATION

RESORT HOTELS

Belmont Hotel and Golf Club $$-$$$
97 Middle Road, Warwick
☎ 236-1301 or US and Canada 1-800-225-5843
A comfortable hotel set in a private 110 acre (44 hectare) hillside estate overlooking Hamilton Harbour and Great Sound. There are 151 large rooms and suites.

Elbow Beach Hotel $$$

PO Box HM 455, Hamilton
☎ 236-3535 or from US 1-800-223-7434

A stunning luxury beachside Rafael Hotel's resort set in 50 acres (20 hectares) of tropical gardens with 294 rooms and suites in the main building and cottages, alongside a beautiful expanse of private pink sand beach.

Grotto Bay Beach Hotel and Tennis Club $$$

11 Blue Hole Hill, Hamilton
☎ 293-8333, USA 1-800-582-3190, Canada 1-800-463-0851

The resort is situated among 21 lush acres (8 hectares) of hibiscus, oleander and bougainvillea gardens along the water's edge with private beach featuring two secluded coves in a sheltered bay. There are 201 rooms and suites in 11 separate lodges, all with private patios or balconies offering sea views.

Hamilton Princess Hotel $$$

PO Box HM 837, Hamilton
☎ 925-3000 or 1-800-223-1818 (US) and 1-800-268-7176 (Canada).

Classic European elegance with Bermudian style and atmosphere. This large, luxury 447 room resort sits on the edge of Hamilton Harbour and offers complete exchange facilities with its sister hotel, the Southampton Princess. There is a Concierge floor for business travelers. Facilities include ferry transportation to the Southampton Princess Beach Club, large freshwater heated pool and patio, smaller saltwater pool, putting green, shopping arcade, beauty salon and fitness facility.

Marriott's Castle Harbour Resort $$$

PO Box HM 841, Hamilton
☎ 293-2040, or 1-800-223-6388 (US and Canada)

A classic Bermuda resort stunning both for its architecture and its location. The 402 room and suite hotel nestles atop a small hill in 250 manicured acres (100 hectares) which run down to the water's edge. The resort is bounded by the world-famous Castle Harbour Golf Club, Castle Harbour and Harrington Sound and spectacular beaches. The views are breathtaking.

Sonesta Beach Hotel and Spa

PO Box HM 1070, Hamilton
☎ 238-8122 and 1-800-SONESTA (US)

A modern, luxury 403 room

115

resort hotel with stunning views and 25 acres (10 hectares) of lovely, landscaped gardens surrounded by three natural bays in Southampton Parish.

Southampton Princess Hotel

PO Box HM 1379, Hamilton
☎ 238-8000 and 1-800-223-1818 (US) and 1-800-268-7176 (Canada).
Standing atop Bermuda's highest point and offering panoramic views across the island, the 600 room luxury resort is surrounded by a golf course and gardens which run down to the water's edge.

SMALL HOTELS

Hamiltonian Hotel and Island Club $$

PO Box HM 1738, Hamilton
☎ 295-5608 and 1-800-441-7087 (US and Canada)
The hotel stands on Langton Hill in tropical gardens, and the 32 one bedroom suites overlook Hamilton and the ocean. There is a large outdoor pool and sundeck, floodlit tennis and nearby golf.

Harmony Club

PO Box PG 299, Paget
☎ 236-3500 and 1-800-225-5843
A luxury all inclusive hotel with 71 spacious, well appointed rooms overlooking the tropical gardens. It is close to the South Shore and a five minute drive from Hamilton.

Mermaid Beach Club

PO Box WK 250, Warwick
☎ 236-5031 and 1-800-441-7097 (US and Canada)
On the ocean side of South Road and offering informal accommodation overlooking the ocean and its own private beach. All 73 rooms and suites have balconies or patios with ocean view.

Newstead

PO Box PG 196, Paget
☎ 236-6060 and 1-800-468-4111 (US)
On Harbour Road and overlooking Hamilton Harbour, this Bermuda manor has 49 modern rooms and cottages set in well groomed grounds and gardens in a quiet residential area.

Palm Reef Hotel

PO Box HM 1189, Hamilton
☎ 236-1000 or 1-800-221-1294 (US and Canada)
This 60 room hotel is centrally located at the water's edge in Paget Parish overlooking Hamilton Harbour and next to the ferry dock.

Palmetto Hotel and Cottages

PO Box FL54, Flatts
☎ 293-2323 or 1-800-982-0026 (US)

A comfortable 42 room property in Flatts Village in Smith's Parish based around an old Bermuda mansion with waterfront cottages.

Pompano Beach Club

36 Pompano Beach Road, Southampton
☎ 234-0222 and 1-800-343-4155 (US and Canada)

On the southwest shore overlooking the ocean with great views from the main clubhouse and all 54 guest rooms.

The Reefs

56 South Road, Southampton
☎ 238-0222 and 1-800-742-2008 (US and Canada)

A lovely 65 room resort on the hill overlooking Christian Bay and its own private beach. All rooms and cottages are set on terraced levels between the beach and the clubhouse, and all have ocean views.

Rosedon $$

PO Box HM 290
☎ 295-1640 and 1-800-225-5567 (US)

On the outskirts of Hamilton in Pembroke Parish, this elegant white Colonial mansion has a wide veran-dah overlooking the lovely gardens. The house has two large lounges and self service bar, and there are 100 spacious rooms in the main house and modern poolside units.

Royal Palms Hotel and Restaurant

PO Box HM 499, Hamilton
☎ 292-1854 and 1-800-678-0783 (US) and 1-800-799-0824 (Canada)

A charming and intimate family run hotel in a unique turn of the century property set among palms and tropical flowers and terraced gardens, in a quiet residential area.

Stonington Beach Hotel

PO Box HM 523, Hamilton
☎ 236-5416 and 1-800-447-7462 (US and Canada)

The hotel is operated by the Hospitality and Culinary Institute of Bermuda overlooking the South Shore in Paget Parish with 64 rooms with terraces or balconies overlooking the ocean and secluded private beach.

Waterloo House

PO Box HM333, Hamilton
☎ 295-4480 and 1-800-468-4100 (US)

A small hotel, formerly an 1800s manor house, in Pembroke Parish with secluded gardens and

attractive courtyard, a three minute walk from downtown Hamilton and the ferry.

White Sands and Cottages

PO Box PG174, Paget
☎ 236-2023 and 1-800-548-0547

A small, intimate property overlooking Grape Bay on the south shore of Paget Parish and a three minute walk to the beach. The buildings are set in well tended gardens with outdoor terrace overlooking the ocean and the beach which is a three minute walk away.

Willowbank

PO Box MA 296, Sandys
☎ 234-1616 and 1-800-752-8493 (US) and 1-800-463-8444 (Canada)

A family hotel by the ocean's edge at Elys Harbour, with the emphasis on spiritual and physical rest. There are 65 rooms in single story units throughout the 6 acres (2.5 hectares) of gardens surrounded on two sides by secluded pink sand beaches.

Cottage Colonies

Ariel Sands Beach Club
PO Box HM334, Hamilton
☎ 236-1010 and 1-800-468-6610, and 1-800-637-4116 (US) and 1-800-267-7600 (Canada)

A secluded cottage colony by the waterside off South Road in Devonshire. The central main clubhouse has large lounge and fireplace, cocktail lounge, bar, dining room and terrace, all with panoramic views, and there are 51 rooms in units spread through the grounds.

Cambridge Beaches

Somerset
☎ 234-0331 and 1-800-468-7300 (US), and 1-800-463-5990 (Canada)

An exclusive 75 room cottage colony set in 25 acres (10 hectares) of beautiful gardens on a peninsula overlooking Mangrove and Long Bays. There are five private beaches, privacy and luxury and an atmosphere of casual elegance.

Fourways Inn

PO Box PG 294, Paget
☎ 236-6517 and 1-800-962-7654 (US)

The house dates from 1727 and was for two centuries the home of the Harvey family, and got its name because there were originally four entrances on to the estate. The coral stone and cedar house has been beautifully restored and renovated and retains great charm and atmosphere.

Horizons and Cottages

PO Box PG 198, Paget

☎ 236-0048

A lovely old Bermuda farmhouse with cottages dotted across the 20 acres (8 hectares) of grounds and gardens overlooking Coral Beach Club and ocean. The main house has two lounges, dining room, bar, cocktail lounge and there are 50 spacious rooms available.

Pink Beach Club and Cottages

PO Box HM 1017, Hamilton

☎ 293-1666 and 1-800-355-6161 (US and Canada)

This cottage colony was founded in 1947 and features two pink sand beaches with guest cottages and 81 rooms nestled in clusters around 18 acres (7 hectares) of natural gardens.

The St George's Club

PO Box GR92, St George's

☎ 297-1200

A full service cottage colony on Rose Hill, St George's, set in 18 acres (7 hectares) of landscaped ground.

PRIVATE CLUBS

Coral Beach and Tennis Club

34 South Road, Paget

☎ 236-2233

Traditional Bermuda cottages, suites and rooms with private terraces on a large oceanfront estate and fronted by a large pink sand private beach.

Mid Ocean Club

PO Box HM 1728, Hamilton

☎ 293-0330

An exclusive, luxury private club by the waterside in Tucker's Town. It has 20 compact efficiency units with balcony overlooking Castle Harbour, with three large private stretches of beach with several secluded beach coves.

LARGE HOUSEKEEPING COTTAGES AND APARTMENTS

Angel's Grotto

PO Box HS 81, Smith's

☎ 293-1986 and 1-800-637-4116 (US) and 1-800—267-7600 (Canada)

There are 7 self contained housekeeping units overlooking Harrington Sound with private access for snorkeling and swimming.

Astwood Cove

49 South Road, Warwick

☎ 236-0984

There are 20 modern, bright attractively furnished studio apartments.

Brightside Apartments

PO Box FL319, Smith's

☎ 292-8410

There are 11 self contained

one and two bedroom units with verandahs in Flatts Village overlooking Flatts Inlet and next to the Bermuda Aquarium, Museum and Zoo.

Clairfont Apartments
PO Box WK 85, Warwick
☎ 238-0149
8 modern, well furnished apartment units each with kitchen, and close to several popular south shore beaches.

The Clear View Suites
Sandy Lane, Hamilton
☎ 293-0484 or 1-800-468-9600 (US)
There are 12 waterfront suites and villas in a quiet residential area, and set in secluded grounds and with lovely ocean views.

Greenbank and Cottages
PO Box PG 201, Paget
☎ 236-3615 and 1-800-637-4116 (US) and 1-800-267-7600 (Canada)
An old Bermuda home and cottages with 11 rooms set in spacious lawns on the water's edge in Salt Kettle.

Longtail Cliffs
PO Box HM836, Hamilton
☎ 236-2864, 1-800-637-4116 (US) and 1-800-267-7600 (Canada)
A scenic location in Warwick Parish with modern two bedroom, two bath-

room apartments all with fully equipped kitchen and overlooking the ocean.

Marley Beach Cottages
PO Box PG 278, Paget
☎ 236-1143 ext 46 and 1-800-637-4116
Spacious housekeeping cottage units and studio apartments.

Munro Beach Cottages
PO Box SN 99, Southampton
☎ 234-1175
A secluded seaside resort overlooking its own private beach and small coves at Whitney Bay.

Paraquet Guest Apartments
PO Box PG 173, Paget
☎ 236-5842
Casual, information accommodation in a residential district with 11 rooms in the main house and adjoining apartment units.

Rosemont
PO Box HM 37, Hamilton
☎ 292-1055 or 1-800-367-0040
Family owned and run with 37 rooms in self contained units on a hillside with views over Hamilton Harbour.

Sandpiper Apartments
PO Box HM 685, Hamilton
☎ 236-7093 and

1-800-441-7087 (US)
Modern, spacious and
informal accommodation in
a residential area of
Warwick Parish. The 14
apartments are fully
equipped with kitchens and
large living room.

Sky Top Cottages
PO Box PG 227, Paget
☎ 236-7984
Set in large gardens of
lawns, flower beds and
citrus trees, the cottages are
fully equipped with English-
style decor. The hilltop
location affords beautiful
views over the surrounding
countryside and ocean
beyond.

Surf Side Beach Club
PO Box WK 101, Warwick
☎ 236-7100 and 1-800-
553-9990 (US)
Overlooking the ocean and
private beach there are 35
cottage apartments on
landscaped terraces. Each
unit is self contained with
kitchen and private porch.

Valley Cottages and Apartments
PO Box PG 214, Paget
☎ 236-0628
Charming informal Bermuda
cottages and self contained
apartments with kitchens or
kitchenettes, patio and
garden areas.

SMALL HOUSEKEEPING COTTAGES AND APARTMENTS

Barnsdale Guest Apartments
PO Box DV 628, Devonshire
☎ 236-0164
There are seven efficiency
studio units each with fully
equipped kitchenettes, in a
private garden area with
pool, and located in a quiet
residential area in Paget
Parish.

Blue Horizons
93 South Road, Warwick
☎ 236-6350
The striking blue house has
6 informal, comfortable
apartment units and guest
bedrooms in a residential
area close to the south
shore beaches.

Burch's Guest Apartments
110 North Shore Road,
Devonshire
☎ 292-5746
A small, informal guest
apartment with 10 self
contained units and pan-
oramic views of the north
shore.

Dawkins Manor
PO Box PG34, Paget
☎ 236-7419
There are 7 comfortable,
housekeeping apartments in
a quiet residential area of
central Paget Parish.

Garden House

4 Middle Road,
Somerset Bridge
☎ 234-1435
A lovely Bermuda property
with an informal, homelike
atmosphere set in 3 acres
(1.2 hectares) of landscaped
gardens in a secluded
location.

Glenmar Holiday Apartments

PO Box PG151, Paget
☎ 236-2844
There are 5 self contained,
efficiency apartments with
kitchens in a residential area
of Paget parish.

Mazarine by the Sea

PO Box HM 91, Hamilton
☎ 292-1659 and
1-800-441-7087 (US)
A small, modern guest
house with 7 rooms on the
water's edge on north shore
in Pembroke parish.

Pillar-Ville Guest House

PO Box SN2, Southampton
☎ 238-0445/0489
A comfortable, informal
guest house on the south
shore and overlooking the
ocean, with 7 rooms and
kitchen facilities.

Vienna Guest Apartments

63 Cedar Hill, Warwick
☎ 236-3300 and
1-800-637-4116 (US) and
1-800-267-7600 (Canada)
A cheerful, family-run guest

house with 6 apartments
with fully equipped kitchen
and panoramic views.

Whale Bay Inn

PO Box SN 544,
Southampton
☎ 238-0469
A well appointed property
overlooking the Port Royal
Golf Course and Whale Bay,
with 5 apartments.

LARGE GUEST HOUSES

Fordham Hall

PO Box HM 692,
Hamilton
☎ 295-1551 and
1-800-537-4163 (US)
A wonderful large house on
Pitts Bay Road in Pembroke
Parish with 12 bedrooms.

Loughlands Guest House

79 South Road, Paget
☎ 236-1253
A lovely, stately white
Beruda mansion set in 9
acres (3.6 hectares) of
gardens, in the middle of
the island yet close to the
south shore beaches.

Oxford House

PO Box HM 374,
Hamilton
☎ 295-0503 and
1-800-548-7758 (US)
This elegant house has 12
large, gracious rooms with
private bathroom.

SMALL GUEST HOUSES

Aunt Nea's at Hillcrest
PO Box GR 96, St George's
☎ 297-1630
A very attractive and comfortable Bermuda home nestled in historic St George's with 11 rooms.

Canada Villa
PO Box HM 1864, Hamilton
☎ 292-0419
A lovely old Bermuda home, offers informal accommodation in 5 comfortable rooms.

Edgehill Manor
PO Box HM 1048, Hamilton
☎ 295-7124
A well appointed, completely refurbished and redecorated old Bermuda home. There are 9 rooms, most with private balcony or terrace.

Garden House
Somerset Bridge, Sandys
☎ 234-1435
A small, informal guest house with five rooms. On the bus route.

Greene's Guest House
PO Box SN 395, Southampton
☎ 238-0834/2113
A modern home in Southampton parish with beautiful ocean views of Great Sound. There are 6 guest rooms with private bath.

Hi-Roy
22 Princess Estate Road, Pembroke
☎ 292-0808
A small modern guest house located in a quiet residential area just off North Shore Road with ocean views.

Little Pomander Guest House
PO Box HM 384, Hamilton
☎ 236-7635
Two tastefully decorated waterfront Bermuda cottages on Hamilton Harbour.

Pleasant View Guest House
PO Box HM 1998, Hamilton
☎ 292-4520
A small, modern guest house in the residential Princess Estate in Pembroke parish, just off North Shore Road.

Que Sera
PO Box HM 1, Hamilton
☎ 236-1998
A small, attractive guest house close to the Botanical Gardens in Paget parish.

Royal Heights Guest House
PO Box SN 144, Southampton
☎ 238-0043
A small, modern guest house with 6 rooms.

AIRLINES/AIRPORTS

The International Airport is the Civil Air Terminal in St George's ☎ 293-1640. It is 9 miles (14km) from Hamilton and 17 miles (27km) from the Somerset and the west end of the island.

AIRLINES

Air Canada	☎ 293-1777 and ☎ 1-800-776-3000
American Airlines	☎ 293-1420 and ☎ 1-800-433-7300
British Airways	☎ 1-800-AIRWAYS and ☎ 0208-897-4000 (UK)
Condor	☎ (49) 6107-939880 (Germany)
Continental	☎ 293-3092 and ☎ 1-800-231-0856
Delta	☎ 1-800-221-1212
SAS	☎ 236-2006
US Airways	☎ 1-800-428-4322 and ☎ 293-3072

AMERICAN EXPRESS

The American Express representative is Meyer Agencies, 35 Church Street, Hamilton ☎ 295-4176.

BANKS

Banks are open Monday to Friday from 9.30am to 3pm, and on Friday additionally from 4.30pm to 5.30pm.
Bank of Bermuda, Head office and Church Street branch ☎ 295-4000.
Bank of Butterfield, Front Street, Hamilton ☎ 295-1111.

BEACHES/SWIMMING

The fabulous pink sand beaches offer safe swimming and it is often possible to have a whole beach to yourselves. The sand gets its hue from the crushed remains of countless millions of shells. Summer sea temperatures reach 85°F (29°C) and the water is stunningly clear and unpolluted.

Tiny Devonshire Bay, Jobson's Cove and Shelly Bay are ideal for novice swimmers and waders, while Tobacco Bay offers great snorkeling. The most popular beaches are Elbow Beach, Warwick Long Bay Beach and the famous Horseshoe Bay Beach.

During the summer, life guards are on duty at Horseshoe Bay Beach and John Smith's Bay during the day. All other public beaches are unguarded. There are no nude or topless beaches on Bermuda.

The following beaches are open to the public without charge:

Achilles Bay	Mangrove Bay
Astwood Park	Margaret's Bay
Black Bay	Parson's Bay
Buildings Bay	Peel Bay
Callaghan Bay	Shelly Bay
Chaplin Bay	Sinky Bay
Church Bay	Somerset Long Bay
Clarence Cove	Spanish Point
Clearwater Beach	Stonehole Bay
Devonshire Bay	Stovell Bay
Elbow Beach	Tobacco Bay
Horseshoe Bay	Turtle Bay
Hungry Bay	Warwick Long Bay
Jobson's Cove	West Whale Bay
John Smith's Bay	Whale Bone Bay

Deep Bay, Fort Hill Bay and Well Bay, all on Cooper's Island off St David's, are also pleasant public beaches.

BICYCLES

Bicycles are fun and a healthy way to get around and a great way to get a tan. The roads are not too hilly and you can always get off and push. The side roads running south to north tend to be the steepest and most twisting. Winds can be strong along the south coast which makes pedaling harder if you are cycling into the wind, but a lot easier if going with it. There are several bike rental shops and many of the resort hotels also have bikes for hire or will arrange it. Costs vary but expect to pay from around $10 to 15 for a day's hire plus $5 to $10 for each day extra.

Bermuda's tropical waters
offer world-class scuba diving

BUSES

The main bus terminal is in Washington Street, Hamilton
☎ 292-3854.

CAR/SCOOTER RENTAL

There is no car rental on Bermuda. Cars were only allowed
on the island for general use in 1946 – and are still limited
to one per household.

Motor scooters and motor assisted bicycles are the most
popular way of getting around, they are more suited to
some of the narrow roads and are easy to park and can
even be used on the beach in some areas. They can be
rented by the half day, day, week and longer. You must be
16 or over to rent a scooter although a driving license is not
required. By law, both drivers and passengers must wear a
safety helmet. Bicycles and tandems can also be rented.
Mopeds cost from $25 a day and $100-120 a week, and
scooters from $35 a day and from $180 a week. Fuel cost is
just under $5 a gallon.

RULES OF THE ROAD

DRIVE ON THE LEFT and observe the speed limit of 20mph
(35kph). At roundabouts, give way to traffic on your
immediate right. Pedestrian crossings are indicated by black
and white stripes across the road and motorists must give
way if someone is crossing. In Hamilton, pedestrians do not
have right of way at traffic lights unless the green pedestrian light is illuminated and the warning bell is ringing.

A single yellow line indicates 'no parking'.

Driving under the influence of alcohol or drugs is against
the law, even on a scooter, and there are heavy penalties if
convicted, especially if it resulted in an accident. Accidents
are not uncommon and more often than not are the result of
inexperienced scooterists going too fast, not braking early
enough and not sticking to the correct side of the road.
Having said that, however, it is not difficult to master these
machines and there should never be any need to speed. If
you are caught in a downpour find a bus shelter until the
rain stops. Rain rarely lasts long and the wind and the sun
will quickly dry your clothes.

If you have an accident or breakdown during the day, call your rental company so make sure you have the telephone number with you. They will usually send out a mechanic or a replacement machine. If you are stuck at night make sure the scooter is off the road and as secure as possible, call a taxi to take you back to your hotel. Report the problem as soon as possible.

Filling stations are open 7am to 7pm daily with some open until 11pm or later.

MAIN SCOOTER/CYCLE RENTAL COMPANIES

Devil's Hole Cycles,
Harrington Sound Road,
Smith's ☎ 293-1280

Dowling's Cycles,
26 York Street, St George's
☎ 297-1614

Eve's Cycle Livery, Middle
Road, Paget ☎ 236-6247.

Oleander Cycles,
Valley Road, Paget
☎ 236-5235, Gorham Road,
Hamilton ☎ 295-0919 and
Middle Road, Southampton
☎ 234-0629

St George's Cycles,
Water Street, St George's
☎ 297-1463

CAVES

Bermuda has one of the highest concentrations of limestone caves in the world. Many of the cave's origins date back to the Pleistocene era and by the time the first English settlers started to explore the island, there were hundreds of huge caverns with their impressive limestone formations of stalactites and stalagmites. When Capt. John Smith recorded his explorations of the island in 1623, he wrote he had found many "strange, darke and cumbersome caves". Two of the largest of the 110 named caves, Crystal Caves and Leamington Caves, both on the Harrington Sound Road, are easily accessible while expert tours of others can be arranged for experienced cavers.

CHURCHES

There are more than 90 churches and houses of worship on the island – more per square mile than anywhere else on earth. Just over a third of the population belong to the Church of England and other denominations, while other faiths represented include Roman Catholic, African

Methodist Episcopal, Pentacostal, Baha'i, Methodist and Seventh Day Adventist.

Anglican Cathedral Diocesan Office	☎ 292-6987
St Theresa's Roman Catholic Cathedral	☎ 292-0607
Baptist Churches	☎ 295-6555
Methodist churches	☎ 292-0418
Seventh Day Adventists	☎ 292-4110
Salvation Army	☎ 292-0601

CLOTHING

Casual, comfortable and conservative are the keywords but you can generally be as smart or as cool as you like – within limits. Bermuda is noted for its British reserve and dignified informality, and there are certain 'customs' of dress.

Beachwear is fine for the beach and pool areas, but cover up on your way to and from, even in public areas of hotels. Bare feet are not considered acceptable anywhere in public, and it is an offence to ride cycles or appear in public without a shirt or just wearing a bathing suit top.

Casual sports wear is acceptable in most restaurants at lunch time, but many restaurants and night clubs require men to wear jacket and tie in the evenings and women can be as elegant as they wish. It is best to check about dress codes when making a dinner or nightclub reservation.

WHAT TO PACK

Warmer months – summer weight sports clothes, swim-suits, raincoat or lightweight wind breaker, and for evening wear for the ladies, casual, elegant cottons, light dressy sweater and cocktail type outfits, while men should have jacket, collar shirts and tie.

Cooler months – Light woolens and casuals, sweater, raincoat and warmer jacket. For the evenings, ladies should pack casual, elegant lightweight woolens, dressier sweater or wrap and cocktail type outfits, while men should have a suit, sports jacket and tie.

If you plan to explore on foot, stout footwear and a good waterproof jacket are essential. Also, wear sunglasses and a hat to protect you from the sun during the hottest part of the day, and you will need sandals on the beach as the sand can get too hot to walk in bare feet.

Bermuda Shorts: The official dress for Bermudian businessmen worn with knee-length Bermuda socks. Formal colors are gray, beige and navy blue while less conservative dressers now opt for brighter colors such as green and pink. Ironically, Bermuda shorts did not develop in Bermuda but in British army camps in the tropics at the turn of the century. Troops were so hot in their long trousers that they cut them off at the knees. Today's Bermuda shorts are best bought from specialist tailors.

CURRENCY

The official currency on the island is the Bermuda dollar which is pegged to the US dollar on a one for one basis. This means that US dollars are accepted everywhere on the islands, and change can be given in either or both currencies.

Other currencies are not accepted but can be exchanged at local banks at rates that are set daily. The banks offer a fixed rate of exchange which is usually better than that offered by hotels. US travelers checks are also widely accepted, and all major credit cards can be used in hotels, dive and watersports operators, many stores and restaurants, and can be used for cash advances at all local bank branches. In addition, there are a number of ATM machines, most of them available round the clock.

Note: Always have a few small denomination notes for tips.

DEPARTURE TAX

There is a $20 departure tax for all air passengers which is collected at the airport, and a $20 voucher can be purchased in advance at many hotels and guest houses.

All ship passengers pay a $60 arrival tax which is normally collected in advance by the cruise ship company.

Children under the age of 2 are exempt from either tax.

DISABLED FACILITIES

Many of the watersports and dive operations will accommodate disabled visitors. There are some facilities for the disabled at most of the larger resorts. A free booklet **Access Guide to Bermuda for the Handicapped Traveller**, is available from Bermuda tourist offices. The Bermuda

Physically Handicapped Association can be contacted on
☎ 292-5025.

DRUGS

There are strict laws prohibiting the importation, possession
and use of drugs, including marijuana. Heavy fines, long
prison sentences or both await those who ignore the law.
If bringing prescription drugs with you, it is prudent to have
a letter from your doctor stating why they have been
prescribed.

ELECTRICITY

The usual electricity supply is 110 volts, 60 cycles AC, the
same as in the US. Adapters are necessary for European
appliances without dual voltages, and these are sometimes
available from hotel guest services or can be bought.

EMBASSIES AND CONSULATES

The following consulates are run by honorary consuls usually
from private offices. If you need to contact one, ring for
advice.

	Office	*Out of hours*
Belgium	☎ 295-2470	☎ 236-6959
Canada	☎ 596-1700	
Germany	☎ 295-2244	☎ 238-3354
Ireland	☎ 028-292-9370	none
Italy	☎ 295-1962	none
Netherlands	☎ 295-4630	☎ 236-0448
Norway	☎ 295-5519	none
Sweden	☎ 292-8369	☎ 295-4789
UK	☎ 292-2587	
US	☎ 295-1342	☎ 295-1342

EMERGENCY TELEPHONE NUMBERS

Police, fire and ambulance ☎ 911
Air sea rescue ☎ 297-1010

ESSENTIAL THINGS TO PACK

Sun block cream, sunglasses, sun hat, camera (and lots of film), insect repellant, binoculars if interested in bird watching and wildlife, and a small torch in case of power failures.

FESTIVALS/PUBLIC HOLIDAYS *

Public holidays * which fall on a weekend are normally observed the following Monday.

January

New Year's Day *
ADT Bermuda Race Weekend attracting an international athletics field
Bermuda Senior Golf Classic
Annual Regional Bridge Tournament
Bermuda Festival – with classical music, dance, jazz, drama and popular entertainment, and continuing into February

February

Lobster Pot Invitational Amateur Golf Tournament Bermuda Amateur Golf Festival
Bermuda Valentine's Mixed Foursomes Invitational
Spittal Pond Children's Nature Walk

March

Bermuda All Breed Championship Dog Shows
Annual Street Festival, Front Street, Hamilton
Bermuda Spring Break Programme

Bermuda Cat Fanciers Association Championship Cat Show
Palm Sunday Walk organized by the Bermuda National Trust
Bermuda Easter Lily Pro-Am Golf Tournament for Ladies

April

Good Friday *(date varies) Church services, kite flying, hot cross buns and codfish cakes
Easter Monday (date varies)
Bermuda Open Tennis Championship
Open Houses and Gardens every Wednesday afternoon
Agriculture Show
Peppercorn Ceremony, St George, when the Masonic Lodge of Bermuda pays its annual peppercorn rent for its headquarters, the Old State House

May

Beating Retreat Ceremonies, alternating between St George's and the Royal

Naval Dockyard, and continuing to October except in August

Invitational International Race Week

International Rugby Classic

TransAt Daytona Bermuda Race (odd years only)

Bermuda Day * (around the 24th) events include the Heritage Day Classic Cycle Race, Annual Bermuda Day Half-Marathon, Bermuda Day Parade and Bermuda Fitted Dinghy Races

June

President's Choice Open Air Pops Concert by the Bermuda Philharmonic Society

Bermuda 1-2 Single Handed Race – (odd years) the event involves a single handed race from Newport to Bermuda with the return leg double-handed

Newport to Bermuda Yacht Race (even years) – a blue water classic

Bermuda Ocean Race (even years)

Bermuda Cruising Rally

Queen's Birthday * (date of the public holiday varies) with military parade on Front Street, Hamilton

July

Cup Match Cricket Festival and **Somers Day*** (a two day public holiday, date varies)

SOCA Concert, Royal Naval Dockyard

Bermuda Angler's Club

International Light Tackle Tournament

August

Somers Day * (date varies)

Bermuda Reggae Sunsplash – featuring local and Jamaican talent

September

Bermuda Horse and Pony Association Fall Show

Labour Day *

October

Annual Bermuda Triathlon

Omega Gold Cup International Match Racing Championship – yachting

November

11 November **Remembrance Day***

Convening of Parliament – ceremonial opening by the Governor

Bermuda All Breed Championship Dog Show and Obedience Trails, a week long event

Bermuda Tattoo – history, pomp and ceremony culminating in a spectacular fireworks display

World Rugby Classic

Bermuda Lawn Tennis Club International

December

Bermuda Goodwill Tournament – golf

Santa Claus Parades

25th **Christmas Day** *

26th **Boxing Day** *

New Year's Eve

HEALTH

There are no serious health problems and no vaccinations are required although visitors should take precautions against the strong sun which can ruin your holiday. Hay fever and other plant allergic sufferers have little to worry about. Rag weed in non existent and pollens are quickly blown out to sea. Immunization is not required unless coming from an infected area. All hotels have doctors either resident or on call, and standards of health care are very high.

TANNING SAFELY

The sun is very strong but sea breezes often disguise just how hot it is. If you are not used to the sun, take it carefully for the first two or three days, use a good sun screen with a factor of 15 or higher, and do not sunbathe during the hottest parts of the day. Cover up and wear sunglasses and a sun hat. Sunglasses will protect you against the glare, especially strong on the beach, and sun hats will protect your head.

If you spend a lot of time swimming or scuba diving, take extra care, as you will burn even quicker because of the combination of salt water and sun. And remember that once a T-shirt is wet it affords no protection from the sun. Use sandals on the beach as the sand can get too hot to walk on comfortably. Calamine lotion and preparations containing aloe are both useful in combating sunburn.

IRRITATING INSECTS

Mosquitoes are not much of a problem on or near the beaches because of onshore winds, but they may well bite you as you enjoy an open air evening meal. Use a good insect repellant, particularly if you are planning trips inland.

Sand flies can be a problem on the beach. Despite their tiny size they can give you a nasty bite. Make sure you check the ground carefully before sitting down otherwise you might get bitten by ants, and the bites can itch for days. In very warm water, Portuguese man-of-war jelly fish sometimes gather offshore and occasionally are washed up on the beach. Both in and out of the water they can give a very painful sting and should be avoided.

Note: Drinking water from the tap is safe and bottled mineral and distilled water is widely available.

HOSPITALS

The King Edward VII Memorial Hospital, Point Finger Road, just outside Hamilton, is a modern, air conditioned facility with practitioners and specialists in every field, and a full range of diagnostic equipment. The emergency room is open round the clock. Major insurance company policies are honored although any payments due must be paid in advance. There is a surcharge for non-residents ☎ 236-2345.

HURRICANES

The islands are on the hurricane belt and although 1995 was the most active hurricane season for more than 50 years, the islands escaped largely unscathed.

Hurricane season is between August and early October, with September the most likely month for tropical storms, although thankfully, most of these pass safely well north of the islands. Weather stations track all tropical storms and give considerable warning of likely landfall.

LANGUAGE

The official language spoken is English.

LOST PROPERTY

Report lost property as soon as possible to your hotel or the nearest police station.

MEDIA

The Royal Gazette is Bermuda's only daily newspaper and most major US and foreign papers and magazines are widely available. The Bermuda Sun publishes twice a week, and the Bermuda Mid Ocean News is a weekly. There are 8 radio and three TV channels, plus cable and satellite channels. The TV channels are Channel 7 (an ABC Network affiliate), Channel 9, (a CBS affiliate) and Channel 11, (the

NBC affiliate). Island information can be heard on VSB 1160 between 7am and 12.15pm and the BBC World Service is broadcast between 12.30pm and 7am.

NIGHTLIFE

There is a great choice of entertainment from great dining to live theatre, cabaret, jazz, dancing, Calypso, steel bands and karaoke. Many of the larger hotels and resorts offer live entertainment, and there are bars, dancing, discos and clubs, some of which stay open until 3am. Most nightclubs have a jacket and tie dress code for men, and many night-clubs and discos have an automatic cover charge. For something really exciting, experience a night dive.

During November to March some hotels cut back or cut out their evening entertainment, but visitors are generally welcome at other hotels for dinner, dancing and entertain-ment, and there are always bars, clubs and nightclubs open. Top spots include **The Club**, Bermudiana Road, and **The Oasis**, Front Street, both in Hamilton, for the liveliest discos; the **Gazebo Lounge**, Hamilton Princess, for the best calypso; and the **Clayhouse Inn**, North Shore Road, Devonshire, for the best local entertainers. **Hubie's Bar**, Angle Street, Hamilton, has great Friday night jazz, and the **Bermuda Folk Club** meets monthly, usually at the Old Colony Club, Trott Road, Hamilton ☎ 293-9241.

PERSONAL INSURANCE AND MEDICAL COVER

Make sure you have adequate personal insurance and medical cover. If you need to call out a doctor or have medical treatment, you will probably have to pay for it at the time, so keep all receipts so that you can reclaim on your insurance.

PHARMACIES

There are a number of pharmacies and over the counter medicines are readily available. Visitors on prescribed medication should bring enough to last them for all the trip as pharmacists cannot dispense foreign prescriptions. In an emergency, a local physician may authorize a refill or replacement. Most pharmacies are open from 8am to 6pm

Monday to Saturday with some opening later and on Sunday. They include:

Bermuda Pharmacy,
Church Street, Hamilton
☎ 295-5375

Clarendon Pharmacy,
Bermudiana Road, Hamilton
☎ 295-9137

Collector's Hill Apothecary,
South Shore Road, Smith's
☎ 236-8664 (also open Sunday 2m to 9pm)

Hamilton Pharmacy,
Church Street, Hamilton
☎ 295-7004

Paget Pharmacy,
Rural Hill Plaza,
Middle Road, Paget
☎ 236-2681
(also open Sunday afternoon)

Robertson's Drugstore,
Customs House Square,
Hamilton ☎ 297-1736
(open Sunday 4 to 6pm)

Woodbourne Chemist,
Woodbourne Avenue,
Pembroke
☎ 295-1073

POLICE

Hamilton's Central Police Station is at 42 Parliament Street ☎ 295-0011. **St George's Police Station** is on the corner of Queen Street and Duke of York Street ☎ 297-1122. **Somerset Police Station** is in Somerset Village ☎ 234-1010.

PORTS

The main port is Hamilton while cruise ships call at Hamilton, St George's and the Royal Naval Dockyard.

POST OFFICE

Letters and cards can be posted at any of the red pillar boxes, at parish post offices, hotel mail boxes and the General Post Office at 56 Church Street, Hamilton ☎ 297-7893. It is open Monday to Friday from 8am to 5pm, and Saturday from 8am to noon. Sub post offices are open Monday to Friday only between 8am and 5pm. In St George's the post office is on the corner of Queen and Water Streets ☎ 297-1610. For the Philatelic Bureau, Hamilton General Post Office ☎ 297-7797.

Postcards to the US and Canada require a 60c stamp, and those to the UK should have a 75c stamp.

Airmail leaves and arrives daily. All mail received in the General Post Office in Hamilton by 9.30am will be dispatched the same day.

PUBLIC TOILETS

There are not many rest rooms on the island, but bars, restaurants and hotels have private facilities which can usually be used if you ask politely.

SECURITY

Bermuda has one of the lowest crime rates in the world, but it makes sense like anywhere else, not to walk around wearing expensive items or flashing large sums of money. Secure your valuables as you should anywhere, and do not leave items unattended on the beach or in an unlocked car.

Don't carry around your passport, travelers checks (cheques) or all your money. Keep them secure in your room or in a hotel safety deposit box. It is also a good idea to have photocopies of the information page of your passport, your air ticket and holiday insurance policy. All will help greatly if the originals are lost.

The islanders are genuinely warm and friendly and very laid back, so there is little hard sell and they will go to great lengths to make your visit memorable.

SERVICE CHARGES AND TAXES

There is a Government hotel occupancy tax of 7.25 per cent on all accommodation bills. A 10-15 per cent service charge may also be added to restaurant bills. Menus and tariffs sometimes include these charges so check to make sure they have not been added again. In shops, the price on the label is what you pay.

SHELLS

There is a huge array of shells to be found along the beaches or in the inshore shallow waters. In the interests of conservation, see how many different types of shells you can find – conch, helmet, bonnet, netted olive, Bermuda cone, scallops, Calico clam, Atlantic pearl oyster and many more – enjoy them and leave them for the next beachcomb-ers to enjoy. Never remove live shells.

SHOPPING

Bermuda offers excellent shopping from top name designer clothes, to the best in cloths, fine china and crystal, silver and silks, perfumes and jewelry from around the world. The emphasis is very much on sophisticated shopping in stores offering quality and high levels of service, so prices even when discounted are still generally high. There are gar-ments in British wool, Scottish tartans and Irish linens. You can buy English china, Irish crystal, Italian leather, Swiss watches, French perfumes and Belgium lace, and much more, all generally at prices 25 to 30 per cent cheaper than in Europe and North America.

Bermuda-made goods include arts and crafts – such as banana leaf dolls, pottery, Bermuda cedar-ware, blown glass, candles, fashions and paintings by local artists (see Galleries above) and island fragrances and perfumes. Local produce for a 'taste of Bermuda' include black rum, local liqueurs, sherry peppers, rum cakes, honey, jams, soups and spices, as well as cook books packed with traditional island recipes.

If buying duty free alcohol and tobacco to take home, you **should purchase them at least 24 hours before depar-ture**. The goods will then be delivered either to the airport or the cruise ship for collection immediately prior to departure.

The main shopping complexes are in Hamilton and St George's. There are some shopping opportunities in Somerset Village and far more in the Royal Naval Dockyard with its Clocktower and Victorian shopping arcades. There are also small shopping arcades in many of the larger hotels. In Hamilton, the main shops are along Front Street which has a number of shopping arcades and alleys packed with boutiques running off it, and Queen Street which has the Windsor Place Mall. Trimingham's on Front Street is the island's largest and oldest department store while the UK chain Marks and Spencer has a store in Reid Street. In St George's the best shopping is on Water Street, Duke of York Street and Somers Wharf.

Shops are open Monday to Saturday from 9am to 5pm, but some stores in Hamilton stay open later if a cruise ship is on port, and on Wednesdays during the summer as part of the Harbour Nights programme.

SIGHTSEEING/TOURS

Sightseeing and island tours by land or sea can be organized through hotels, tour representatives or one of the many destination management and specialist tour companies on the island. These include:

Bee-Line Transportation, PO Box HM 2270, Hamilton ☎ 293-0303

Bermuda Hosts, PO Box CR 46, Hamilton Parish ☎ 293-1334

Bermuda Island Cruises, PO Box HM 2249, Hamilton ☎ 292-8652

Bermuda Meetings and Incentives, PO Box CR63, Hamilton ☎ 293-8429

BIU Taxi Co-op Transportation, Astor House, 40 Union Street, Hamilton ☎ 292-4476

Butterfield Travel, PO Box HM 656, Hamilton ☎ 292-1510

Destination Bermuda, PO Box HM 1822, Hamilton ☎ 292-2325

L.P. Gutteridge Hospitality Management, PO Box HM 1024, Hamilton ☎ 295-4545

Penboss Destination Management, PO Box 510, Hamilton ☎ 295-9733

Tam-Marina of Bermuda, Jonathan's Landing, 61 Harbour Road, Paget ☎ 236-0127

Trott Travel, PO Box HM 721, Hamilton ☎ 295-0041

For boat trips contact:

Andrea Christine Charters ☎ 295-1240

Argo Adventures ☎ 297-1439

Bermuda Belle ☎ 235-1492

Bermuda Island Cruises ☎ 292-8652

Bermuda Longtail New ☎ 292-0282

Bermuda Water Tours ☎ 295-3727

Champagne Cruises ☎ 236-7435

Coral Sea Cruises ☎ 236-7637

Fantasea Cruises ☎ 236-6339

Jesse James Cruises ☎ 236-4804

Looking Glass Cruises ☎ 295-0460

Somerset Bridge Cruises ☎ 234-2738

SPORT

Because of the strong British tradition, cricket, rugby and soccer are all played, as well as golf and tennis. Cricket is played with a passion and there is great rivalry between teams, especially the Somerset and St George's cricket clubs which have been competing against each other since 1902. There are Sunday matches throughout the summer. The two day annual Cup Match held at the Somerset Cricket Club ground off Somerset Road, on the Thursday and Friday before the first Monday in August attracts such large crowds that both days have been declared national holidays, ensuring that people don't have to think up excuses for missing work!

Local rugby, hockey and football teams battle it out during weekends between September and April – rugby matches are normally played on Saturday afternoons, soccer matches on Sunday afternoon and hockey on alternate weekends. The National Sports Stadium, Middle Road, Devonshire, is the venue for hockey and rugby over the winter and hosts many visiting club and international teams.

Basketball and baseball are both popular with islanders – a legacy of the US Armed Forces stationed on Bermuda.

OTHER SPORTS

For the visitor, there is a huge range of sporting opportunities from swimming and scuba diving, to hiking and tennis, or having a game of cricket with one of the local teams. There is boating, cycling, golf, sailing, squash, water skiing, parasailing, horseback riding and, of course, fishing either from shore or boat.

Most hotels offer a variety of sports and water activities, and dive operators offer all level of instruction. You can learn what it is all about and progress to advanced level if you have the time.

Walking is great fun and there are lots of trails but have stout, non-slip footwear and a waterproof. Protect yourself against insects, carry adequate drinking water and keep an eye on the time, because night falls quickly and you don't want to be caught out on the trail after dark.

CYCLING

On an island where there are no rental cars, bikes are a good way of getting around, getting a tan and working off all the great food. Some hotels provide cycles for guests, but they are readily available for rent. In fact, cycling has been a way of life on Bermuda since 'bone shakers' were introduced in the 19th century. The bikes got their names because in those days, the roads were made with crushed rocks. Today's smooth roads and trails make cycling a pleasure and, if you don't want to pedal, you can even rent a motor assisted bike to do the work for you. At weekends you can usually join in with one of the informal cycling groups.

Bermuda Bicycle Association, 22 Ewing Street, Hamilton ☎ 292-9175

FITNESS GYMS/HEALTH CENTERS

Many of the main hotels and resorts offer health and fitness facilities. Others include:

Apples Fitness Centre, 70 Somerset Road, Somerset ☎ 234-2534

The Athletics Club, Cedarparkade, Hamilton ☎ 295-6140

Bersalon Salon and Spas, Front Street West, Hamilton, and Water Street, St George's, for information ☎ 292-8570

Magnum Power Force Gym, 119 Front Street, Hamilton ☎ 292-7007

The Olympic Club, 13 Dundonald Street, Hamilton ☎ 292-4095

Total Fitness Centre, 24 Brunswick Street, Hamilton ☎ 295-0087

FISHING

Fishing is an island pursuit, and many islanders will fish for hours from quay walls, beach and boats. With more than 650 species of fish, there is year-round world-class deep sea and game fishing, especially off the Argus and Challenger Banks. Species include Atlantic blue marlin, white marlin, skipjack, blackfin and yellowfin tuna, also called allison and can weigh over 100lbs (45kg), wahoo, little tunny, amberjack, rainbow runner, great barracuda and white marlin (which can weigh more than 100lbs) and the fighting sailfish. Dolphin, is a popular catch, and is also called dorado and mahi-mahi (it is a fish and not the mammal). Blue marlin regularly weigh in at between 300 and 500lbs (136–226kg), although fish weighing more than 1,000lbs (454kg) have been caught. Snapper, bonefish, permit, pompano (palometa), mackerel, tarpon, grouper, bonito and barracuda can all be caught close to shore, while over the reefs, favorite catches are yellowtail snapper, greater amberjack, almaco jack, great barracuda, little tunny, gray snapper, yellow tail snapper and Bermuda chub. Mako, blue, tiger and hammerhead are among the several species of shark that can be found off the islands. Around the reefs there is an abundance of grouper, jack crevalle, mutton snapper and yellowtail snapper. While there is year round fishing, the best months are from May to November.

Visitors are encouraged to enter their catches in the year-round game fishing competitions with the Bermuda Department of Tourism. No license is required and there is no entry fee. Awards of Merit, Citations and Outstanding Angling Achievement Awards are presented. Fishermen are encouraged to use the worldwide 'tag and release' scheme.

There are many guides and charter boats for rent. Fishing charter boats are all fully inspected, equipped with rods and all other necessary equipment, fighting chairs and outriggers, and skippered by licensed guides. All have (restroom) facilities. Prices vary enormously depending on the vessel, season, type of fishing requested, and size of the boat. All equipment is provided except food and refreshments. Before chartering, discuss the policy of the skipper regarding landed fish. Does the boat retain all or some of the catch; can you choose which fish you want; does the boat operate the tag and release policy?

Boats can be charted for half a day (4 hours) or a full day (8 hours), but bear in mind that if there is a long journey to and from the fishing ground a half day's rental might not offer too much time for fishing.

Bermuda Game Fishing Association, PO Box HM 1306, Hamilton.

Fishing equipment can be rented from:

Four Winds Fishing Tackle,
2 Woodlands Road,
Pembroke ☎ 292-7466

Mangrove Marina, end of
Cambridge Road, Mangrove
Bay, Somerset ☎ 234-0914

GOLF

The island has two nine hole and seven 18-hole courses –
more per square mile than any other country in the world!
All the courses are memorable in more ways than one. They
offer year-round golf, spectacular scenery and sweeping
views, and many of the courses are surrounded by the
island's famous pink sand beaches with the turquoise seas
and emerald reefs beyond. A new Jack Nicklaus-designed
course is under construction on the 250-acre (101 hectares)
former US Naval Annex in Southampton Parish.

Apart from your clubs, a camera and lots of film should be
essential parts of your golf equipment. The courses also
offers challenges that can daunt the most competent golfer.
The wind is the main problem because conditions are rarely
the same two days running and gusts can carry the ball off
course. This is not a place to slice your shots as the ball
could easily end up in the ocean.

Golf is taken very seriously on the island, and while
playing is fun, all the clubs have dress codes and insist on
punctual starting times. Proper golf attire is required. Shirts
must have collars and sleeves, and smart shorts must be at
least Bermuda length. Jeans and cut-offs are not allowed.
Starting times must be arranged in advance and kept. Golf
clubs can be rented at all the courses.

St George's Club

The **St George's Club**, on the east end of the island, is the
newest of Bermuda's Government golf courses. The 4,502
yard (4117m), par 64 course was designed by Robert Trent
Jones, and although the holes are short – one par five, eight
fours and nine threes – they are tricky and downright
difficult if the wind is strong. The views are stunning, the
golf challenging – and the best photo opportunities on the
7th, 8th and 15th holes!

Castle Harbour Resort

Around Harrington Sound, a beautiful inland lake connected
to the sea by a narrow channel, is Castle Harbour Resort
and Bermuda's oldest and most famous course, the Mid
Ocean Club.

The **Castle Harbour** course needs a lot of concentration
because of the stunning views and the steep drops, banks

and hills that test your skill as well as your courage. Leaving the clubhouse to play the first hole offers an amazing panorama over Castle Harbour's blue green waters. The undulating 6,440 yard (5889m), par 71 course was designed by Charles Banks and Robert Trent Jones.

The **Mid Ocean Club** is private but non members can play if introduced by a hotel or member. The 6,547 yard (5986m), par 71 course is situated in exclusive TuckersTown and famous players over the years have included the Duke of Windsor, Dwight D. Eisenhower and Winston Churchill. The fifth hole, Mangrove Lake is renowned for being one of the best in the world.

Another 5 miles (8km) or so west lies the island's only nine hole course **Ocean View**. The 2,956 yard (2703m), par 35 course, is in Devonshire Parish in the middle of the island, and owned and maintained by the government. The course is not as easy as it looks because of its unpredictable terrain and hills, and the fantastic sea views from the elevated greens are another distraction.

The **Belmont Hotel and Country Club** is close to Hamilton. The 5,777 yard (5282m), par 70 course is compact and only one par 4 exceeds 400 yards (366m), but it is very challenging. Most of the fairways are tight with elevated and double tiered greens, blind second shots and small, narrow greens.

Riddells Bay and Golf Club is the only other private golf club although visitors are welcome if they have an introduction from their hotel or a member. The 5,588 yard (5110m), par 69 course opened in 1922, and is set on a remarkably narrow peninsula which is only 600 yards (549m) across at its widest, so there is no room for slices or hooks. The course is noted for its tight fairways and small, narrow greens and the 8th and 9th holes are both across water.

Overlooking the lovely South Shore beaches is the **Princess Golf Club**, an 'executive' par 3 course which offers a real challenge and anyone breaking 60 has played a great game. The 2,684 yard (2454m) course is packed with hazards from ponds and bunkers to elevated tees.

Horizons, off South Road in Paget parish, is a picturesque 9-hole course.

Finally, the **Port Royal Golf Club** is government-owned and overlooks Southampton's South Shore. The 6,565 yard

(6003m), par 71 course was also designed by Robert Trent Jones and opened in 1972. It is host to the Bermuda Open Championships each October, and is rightly regarded as one of the best public courses in the world.

Belmont Hotel Golf and Country Club, Warwick ☎ 236-1301
Castle Harbour Golf Club, Tucker's Town ☎ 293-0795
Horizons, Paget ☎ 236-0048
Mid Ocean Club, Tucker's Town ☎ 293-0330
Ocean View Golf Course, Devonshire ☎ 236-6758

Port Royal Golf Course, Southampton ☎ 234-0974
Princess Golf Club, Southampton ☎ 238-0446
Riddells Bay Golf and Country Club, Warwick ☎ 238-1060
St George's Golf Club, St George's ☎ 297-8353

HORSE RIDING

With year round good weather, stunning views and bridle paths along both the North and South Shores, it is great place for horse back riding. There are mounts to suit all levels of experience, and even if you have never ridden before, you can head off along a trail on a safe mount accompanied by qualified instructors. Remember to take your camera as the views, especially just after sun up are stunning. Horse riding is available at:

Lee Bow Riding Centre, 1 Tribe Road, Devonshire ☎ 236-4181. Caters to juniors up to 18 and small groups for one hour trail rides.

Spicelands Riding Centre, Middle Road, Warwick ☎ 238-8212. Breakfast, trail and evening rides and lessons for all levels.

JOGGING

Although it is a small island, there are miles of trails and paths to run along. There is the winding Railway Trail, acres of park land, beaches, fun runs round the Botanical Gardens and other events where you can join in with fellow enthusiasts. The Bermuda Striders and Hash House Harriers both meet in Sundays and welcome visitors.

SCUBA DIVING

Bermuda is one of the most fascinating scuba diving destinations anywhere. It boasts the northernmost coral reefs in the world, incredible visibility often up to 150 feet (46m), spectacular marine life and hundreds of wrecks dating back to the 15th century. One of the most famous wrecks is the 200 foot (61m) four masted schooner *Constellation*, which sank in 1943 and was the inspiration for Peter Brenchley's chilling novel *The Deep*. Nearby is the *Montana*, a paddle steamer which sank in 1863. There are shimmering sea fans, beautiful corals and teeming shoals of tropical fish.

There are several fully-equipped dive operators offering training, equipment and a wide range of dives, from wreck and reef dives, to two tank, deep and night dives for experienced divers.

Powerboat and catamaran cruises are available to the offshore reefs.

The waters are near perfect for **snorkeling** and the inshore shallows are safe for young children and non swimmers provided they are supervised. Masks, fins and snorkels are available from charter boats, at many waterside hotels and some beaches. **Note: Spearguns are regarded as firearms under the Firearms Act and their import is banned.**

The Bermuda Sub Aqua Club, is based in Admiralty House Grounds, Spanish Point ☎ 293-9531.

Scuba operators

Blue Water Divers, Robinson's Marina, Somerset Bridge, Sandys ☎ 234-1034. From introductory courses to two tank and night dives.

Dive Bermuda, Dockyard Terrace, PO Box SB 246, Sandys ☎ 234-0225. Reef and wreck dives for certified divers only.

Fantasea Diving, Darrells Wharf, Harbour Road, Paget ☎ 236-6339. Introductory beach or pool courses to two tank, reef, wreck and night dives.

Nautilus Diving, Southampton Princess Hotel, Southampton ☎ 238-2332. Introductory resort courses to reef, wreck and two tank dives. Night dives and other certifications available.

South Side Scuba Water Sports, at Grotto Bay Beach Hotel and Sonesta Beach Hotel and Spa, both ☎ 293-2915. Introductory pool courses to two tank and night dives and certification courses.

Snorkeling operators

Bermuda Barefoot Cruises,
PO Box DV 525, Devonshire
☎ 236-3498.

Bermuda Water Sports,
Grotto Bay Beach Hotel,
Hamilton Parish
☎ 293-8333.

Bermuda Water Tours,
PO Box HM 1572, Hamilton
☎ 295-3727.

Pitman's Snorkeling,
Somerset Bridge Hotel
Dock, Somerset Bridge
☎ 234-0700.

Salt Kettle Boat Rentals, Salt
Kettle, Paget ☎ 236-4863.

Sand Dollar Cruises,
PO Box HM 534, Hamilton
☎ 292-6104.

Watersports Centre, Royal
Naval Dockyard ☎ 234-0250.

Helmet diving is an option for those who want to walk among the reefs but don't have any diving experience. No lessons or swimming skills are needed, and it is great opportunity for children aged 5 and up and non-swimmers to explore the reefs at close quarters. Operators include:

**Bronson Hartley's
Underwater Wonderland**,
Flatts Village, Smith's
☎ 292-4434. Conducted
underwater walks at depths
of 10 to 12 feet (3 to 3.6m)
for anyone from 5-85.
Departs Flatts Village.

**Greg Hartley's Under Sea
Adventure**, PO Box SB 194,
Sandys ☎ 234-28661.
Boat leaves Village Inn
dock in Somerset.

**Peppercorn Diving
Adventures**, Grotto Bay
Hotel ☎ 293-1620.

SQUASH

There are facilities at the **Bermuda Squash and Racquets Club**, Middle Road, Devonshire ☎ 292-6881, and the **Coral Beach and Tennis Club**, South Road, Paget ☎ 236-2233.

TENNIS

Tennis was introduced to Bermuda by Thomas Middleton who visited England in 1871, saw the game being played and returned to the island with all the necessary equipment. He then thought tennis might be too strenuous for his wife so he gave the equipment to his friend Sir Brownlow Gray who had the first court built. His daughter Mary was responsible for tennis becoming the national sport, and in 1872 Mary Outerbridge is said to have introduced the game to America. On returning to New York after a holiday on

Bermuda she persuaded her brother, a director of the Staten Island Cricket Club, to build a court in the grounds.

Today there are more than 100 all-weather courts and several are floodlit. Most hotels have their own facilities and you can also play on public courts. Proper tennis attire is preferred on all courts.

If newly arrived on the island, book a court early in the morning or late in the afternoon when it is cooler until you adjust to the heat.

The following are just some of the locations where you can play:

Coral Beach and Tennis Club, Paget, a private club with professional staff and guest facilities ☎ 236-2233.

Government Tennis Stadium, Pembroke ☎ 292-0105.

Marriott's Castle Harbour Resort, Tucker's Town ☎ 293-2040.

Pomander Gate Tennis Club, Paget ☎ 236-5400.

Port Royal Club, Southampton ☎ 234-0974.

WATER SPORTS AND AQUATIC ACTIVITIES

Available at all resorts and most large hotels and range from Hobie Cats, jet skis, windsurfers, Sunfish, Boston whalers, day sailers and parasailing. You can even rent a mini glass bottomed boat and explore the marine life.

Experts are also on hand to teach you how to sail, water ski and parasail. **Parasailing** is becoming increasingly popular and you don't even have to get your feet wet now if you choose the Skyrider, a two man chair. Although you can soar to 300 feet (91m) into the air, it is completely safe and an unforgettable experience for all ages. You take off from and land on the deck of a boat, and there are parasailing opportunities at Castle Harbour, Great Sound or along South Shore in Southampton.

The many protected Harbours and inland waterways are ideal for **water-skiing,** and water-skiing operators offer lessons for the novice as well as equipment such as trick skis, knee boards, surfers and water sleds for the most experienced skiers. Water-skiers must operate only in designated areas, and always well away from swimmers. You can water-ski year round but the best times are between May and the end of September.

Windsurfing is claimed to be the world's fastest growing sport, and Bermuda's ever present and constantly changing winds, make it an ideal destination for both novices and experienced windsurfers. Best areas are Somerset Long Bay, Horsehoe Bay, Shelly Bay, Castle Harbour, Achilles Bay and almost anywhere along the North Shore. Best times of the year are from October to April. Several operators, specializing in light-wind sailing, are located at hotel marinas, and for first-timers, there are experienced instructors who will have you up and going in no time.

The following offers equipment and lessons:

Boardsailing

Mangrove Marina,
  end of Cambridge Road,
  Mangrove Bay, Somerset
  ☎ 234-0914

**South Side Scuba
  Water Sports**,
  Grotto Bay Beach Hotel,
  Hamilton Parish and
  **Marriott's Castle Harbour
  Resort**, Hamilton Parish,
  both ☎ 293-2915

Para Sailing

Para Sail Bermuda,
  Southampton Princess
  Hotel, Southampton
  ☎ 238-2332

**South Side Scuba
  Water Sports**,
  Marriott's Castle Harbour
  Resort, Hamilton Parish
  ☎ 293-2915

Motor boats

Mangrove Marina,
  end of Cambridge Road,
  Mangrove Bay, Somerset
  ☎ 234-0914

Rance's Boatyard,
  Crow Lane, Paget
  ☎ 292-1843

**Robinson's Charter
  Boat Marina**, Somerset
  Bridge, Sandys ☎ 234-0709

Salt Kettle Boat Rentals,
  Salt Kettle, Paget
  ☎ 236-4863

**South Side Scuba
  Water Sports**, Grotto Bay
  Beach Hotel, Hamilton
  Parish ☎ 293-2915

Sailing lessons

Salt Kettle Boat Rentals,
  Salt Kettle, Paget
  ☎ 236-4863

**South Side Scuba Water
  Sports**, Grotto Bay Beach
  Hotel, Hamilton Parish
  ☎ 293-2915

Water-skiing

Bermuda Waterski Centre,
  Robinson's Marina,
  Somerset Bridge
  ☎ 234-3354/1964

Island Water Skiing,
  Grotto Bay Beach Hotel,
  Hamilton Parish ☎ 293-2915

Watersports Centre,
  Royal Naval Dockyard
  ☎ 234-0250

The Bermuda Race is one of the world's premier challenges for ocean going yachts. The race was first held in 1906 and has been held every two years since 1924, except during the Second World War, and in 1936 the current route was introduced – a 635 mile (1022km) dash from Newport, Rhode Island in the United States to Bermuda. The event is co-sponsored by the Cruising Club of America and the Royal Bermuda Yacht Club, and there are two main awards – one for the fastest cruiser/racer, and the other for the fastest grand prix racer. The race record was established in 1956 when Sven Salen in his yawl *Bolero*, completed the distance in 70 hours and 11 minutes.

Yachts, motor boats and fishing boats are available for charter for day sailing, sightseeing, fishing and diving, and longer trips. Sail yourself boats capable of carrying from one to six people are available, and motorboats can be rented self drive or with skipper.

Marinas

Dockyard Marina, Ireland Island ☎ 234-0300

Mangrove Marina, Cambridge Road, Somerset ☎ 234-0914

Robinson's Marina, Somerset Bridge, Sandys ☎ 234-0709

Skipper yourself and charter Boat rentals

Mangrove Marina, end of Cambridge Road, Mangrove Bay, Somerset ☎ 234-0914

Pompano Beach Club Watersports Centre, 36 Pompano Beach Road, Southampton ☎ 234-0222

Rance's Boatyard, Crow Lane, Paget ☎ 292-1843

Robinson's Charter Boat Marina, Somerset Bridge, Sandys ☎ 234-0709

Salt Kettle Boat Rentals, Salt Kettle, Paget ☎ 236-4863

South Side Scuba Water Sports, Grotto Bay Beach Hotel and Marriott's Castle Harbour Resort, both Hamilton Parish ☎ 293-2915

Charter yachts with licensed skippers

Bermuda Caribbean Yacht Charter, 2a Light House Road, Southampton ☎ 238-8578

Golden Rule Cruise Charters, PO Box SN 581, Southampton ☎ 238-1962

Harbour Island Cruises,
  PO Box HM 2117, Hamilton
  ☎ 234-7245
Longtail Cruises, PO Box HM
  722, Hamilton ☎ 236-4482
Mangrove Marina, end of
  Cambridge Road, Mangrove
  Bay, Somerset ☎ 234-0914
Ocean Yacht Charters,
  PO Box SN109,
  Southampton ☎ 295-1180
Sail Bermuda, c/o Williams
  Marine, PO Box HM 1622,
  Hamilton ☎ 238-0774
Salt Kettle Boat Rentals,
  Salt Kettle, Paget
  ☎ 236-4863
Sand Dollar Cruises,
  PO Box HM 534, Hamilton
  ☎ 292-6104
Starlight Sailing Cruises,
  PO Box HM 622, Hamilton
  ☎ 292-1834

Wind Sail Charters,
  PO Box HM 1699, Hamilton
  ☎ 238-0825

Charter motor yachts with licensed skippers

Bermuda Barefoot Cruises,
  PO Box DV525, Devonshire
  ☎ 236-3498
Bermuda Water Sports,
  PO Box CR 259, Crawl
  ☎ 293-2640
Bermuda Water Tours,
  PO Box HM 1572, Hamilton
  ☎ 295-3727
Jessie James Cruises,
  48 Par la Ville Road, Suite
  366, Hamilton ☎ 236-4804
Salt Kettle Boat Rentals,
  Salt Kettle, Paget
  ☎ 236-4863
Tam Marina, The Lady Boats,
  61 Harbour Road, Paget
  ☎ 236-0127

TELEPHONES

Bermuda has a modern telecommunications system operated by the Bermuda Telephone Company, allowing direct dialing worldwide. Bermuda's area code is 441 followed by the 7 digit local number. Calls to Bermuda from the US are long distance calls, so dial 1-441 followed by the seven digit number. From the UK dial 010 1-441 plus the local number. For directory assistance dial 411.

Most hotels levy a surcharge for long distance and international calls made through their switchboards, even when collect (reverse charge) calls and these can be hefty surcharges. There are AT&T and USA Direct phones at the airport, cruise ship terminal, Dockyard and on Ordnance Island in St George's. Calls to North America are cheaper in the evening. Cable and Wireless, 20 Church Street, Hamilton ☎ 297-7000, can assist with cables, telexes, faxes and overseas calls. The office is open Monday to Friday from 9am to 5pm. Local calls cost 20c.

TIME

Bermuda is in the Atlantic time zone and Bermuda Standard Time is one hour ahead of US Eastern Standard Time and four hours behind Greenwich Mean Time i.e. if it is noon in Hamilton it is 4pm in London and 11am in New York. Bermuda adopts Daylight Saving Time from the first Sunday in April to the last Sunday in October when island time is five hours behind GMT.

TIPPING

Many hotels and guest houses add 10 per cent or a daily amount to your accommodation bill in lieu of tips. This should be pointed out when you check in. In addition, there is a government 7.25 per cent hotel occupancy tax. A 15 per cent service charge is generally added to restaurant bills but if not, it is customary to add this amount if you are satisfied with the food and the service. It is customary to tip taxi drivers and guides, and tipping porters, maids and bellboys is discretionary.

TOURIST OFFICES

The Bermuda Department of Tourism is in Global House, 43 Church Street, Hamilton ☎ 292-0023.

There are Tourist Information Centres in **Hamilton** in the **ferry terminal** on Front Street; **King's Square**, **St George's** (open April to October, Monday to Saturday 9am to 3pm, with curtailed opening November to March); **The Airport** (open to meet most incoming flights); **Royal Naval Dockyard** (open April to October Sunday to Friday 9am to 3pm, with curtailed opening November to March); and **Somerset** (open April to October daily 9am to 3pm, and closed November to March). Information is also available by calling ☎ 295-1480.

Overseas, there are Bermuda tourist offices in:

US ☎ 1-800-223-6106

205 East 42nd Street,
    New York NY 10017
    ☎ 212-818-9800

150 N. Wacker Drive, Suite
    1070, Chicago Il 60606
    ☎ 312-782-5486

245 Peachtree Centre
  Avenue, Suite 803,
  Atlanta GA 30303
  ☎ 404-524-1541
44 School Street, Suite 1010,
  Boston MA 02108
  ☎ 617-742-0405
5208 Sand Point Place NE,
  Suite 3, Seattle WA 98105
  ☎ 206 527-7065

Canada

1200 Bay Street, Suite 1004,
  Toronto, Ontario M5R 2A5
  ☎ 416-923-9600

UK

1 Battersea Church Road,
  London SW11 3LY
  ☎ 0207-734-8813

WEDDINGS

Bermuda is an increasingly popular destination for couples
wishing to get married, and most hotels, cottage colonies
and guest houses offer special wedding and honeymoon
packages and have experts available to help you with all the
planning.

Visitors wishing to get married on Bermuda must have
their 'Notice of Intended Marriage' published in the
Bermuda newspapers. Only those British subjects resident
in the UK who intend to marry a British subject resident
in Bermuda, and for whom banns are called in their
normal place of worship in Britain, can also have their own
banns called in the church where the marriage is to take
place.

No blood tests or health certificates are required, but
copies of final divorce decrees must accompany the 'Notice
of Intended Marriage' form for all divorced persons wishing
to be married in Bermuda.

1 Notice must be given to the Registrar General, Government Administration Building, 30 Parliament Street,
Hamilton HM 12, Bermuda ☎ 441-297-7709/7707 or fax
441-292-4568, either in person or by mail or fax.

2 A 'Notice of Intended Marriage' form must be completed,
including name and residential address in full, and
accompanied by a money order, cashier's check (cheque)
or bank draft for the fee of $150 in Bermuda or US
dollars, and made payable to the Accountant General,
Hamilton, Bermuda. Personal checks (cheques) cannot be
accepted. Notice of Intended Marriage forms can be
obtained from the Bermuda Department of Tourism

offices in New York, Atlanta, Boston, Chicago, Los Angeles, Toronto and London and the office of the Registrar General in Bermuda.

3 The Notice of Intended Marriage is published by the Registry staff in two local newspapers, and a period of 14 days must elapse from the date of receipt of the notice by the Registry before the Registry General may issue the license to marry, provided no formal objections have been lodged. Once issued, the license remains valid for three months.

4 Marriages are performed at the Registry by appointment between 10am and 4pm Monday to Friday, and on Saturday from 10am to noon. Two witnesses are required for Registry marriages. The fee for the Registry marriage is $153 which includes the cost of the ceremony and certificate.

5 If the marriage is to take place in a church or other venue, other fees will be charged in addition to the $17 for the marriage certificate. Outdoor weddings or buildings other than a church can be arranged with the consent of the officiating clergyman.

Note: Divorced people cannot be married in any of the Catholic churches in Bermuda, although church weddings for divorcees can sometimes be arranged by special request with the Minister at other church denominations. And, Catholics not normally resident in Bermuda cannot be married in Catholic Churches in Bermuda except under the most exceptional circumstances.

SPECIALIST WEDDING CONSULTANTS

Bermuda Wedding Associates,
PO Box CR 228, Hamilton Parish CR BX ☎ 441-293-4033

The Bridal Suite,
PO Box SN 96, Southampton SN 96 ☎ 441-238-0818

Special Occasions,
12 North Shore Road, Flatts Village FL04 ☎ 441-292-1217

The Wedding Salon,
51 Reid Street, Hamilton HM 11 ☎ 441-292-5677

• Index •

Index

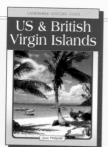

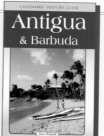
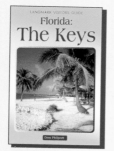

Published in the UK by
Landmark Publishing Ltd,
Waterloo House, 12 Compton, Ashbourne, Derbyshire
DE6 1DA England
Tel: 01335 347349 Fax: 01335 347303 e-mail: landmark@clara.net

Published in the USA by
Hunter Publishing Inc,
130 Campus Drive, Edison NJ 08818
Tel: (732) 225 1900, (800) 255 0343 Fax: (732) 417 0482
Web site: www.hunterpublishing.com

1st Edition
ISBN 1 901 522 07 5

British Library Cataloguing in Publication Data: a catalogue record for this book is available from the British Library.

Print: SunFung Offset Binding Co. Ltd, China
Cartography: James Allsopp
Design: James Allsopp & Samantha Witham

Front Cover: There are many small coves
so you can get away from it all
Back cover, top: Long Bay, Warwick Parish
Back cover, bottom: Bermudian "policeman"
conducts traffic in Hamilton

Picture Credits
Bermuda Tourism: Front Cover, page 3, 118 & 127
All other pictures are supplied by the author